Mary Neal and the Suffragettes Who Saved Morris Dancing

Mary Neal and the Suffragettes Who Saved Morris Dancing

Kathryn Atherton

PEN & SWORD
HISTORY

AN IMPRINT OF PEN & SWORD BOOKS LTD.
YORKSHIRE – PHILADELPHIA

First published in Great Britain in 2024 by
Pen & Sword History
An imprint of
Pen & Sword Books Ltd
Yorkshire - Philadelphia

ISBN 978 1 39906 150 6

A CIP catalogue record for this book is available from the British Library

Typeset in INDIA by IMPEC eSolutions
Printed and bound in the UK by CPI Group (UK) Ltd, Croydon, CR0 4YY

Pen & Sword Books Limited incorporates the imprints of Atlas, Archaeology, Aviation, Discovery, Family History, Fiction, History, Maritime, Military, Military Classics, Politics, Select, Transport, True Crime, Air World, Frontline Publishing, Leo Cooper, Remember When, Seaforth Publishing, The Praetorian Press, Wharncliffe Local History, Wharncliffe Transport, Wharncliffe True Crime and White Owl.

For a complete list of Pen & Sword titles please contact

PEN & SWORD BOOKS LIMITED
47 Church Street, Barnsley, South Yorkshire S70 2AS, United Kingdom
E-mail: enquiries@pen-and-sword.co.uk
Website: www.pen-and-sword.co.uk

or

PEN AND SWORD BOOKS
1950 Lawrence Rd, Havertown, PA 19083, USA
E-mail: Uspen-and-sword@casematepublishers.com
Website: www.penandswordbooks.com

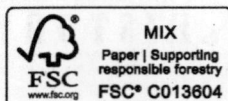

MIX
Paper | Supporting
responsible forestry
FSC
www.fsc.org
FSC® C013604

Contents

One feels she does it all for her own fun, not for the good of her soul, and to join in and really appreciate the lives of those she befriends rather than to 'save' them. She is always an absolutely sound, honest, unposing creature with an abundant sense of humour of the right sort.

Lady Constance Lytton

You have lived in the life of your time and have woven your ideals and your creative work into the fabric of the national community. Your work has been the expression of your spirit; it has been done by the inspiration of your desire and will so that its success has been in a true sense its own reward, and you have been content to forego both financial and public recognition.

Dedication to Mary Neal at a presentation by friends, supporters and admirers in 1925

Acknowledgments and thanks

Thanks are due to many people and organisations who have contributed information, offered contacts and allowed access to their collections. First among them is Brian Butterly who encouraged me to write up years of accumulated material in the depths of the first Covid lockdown and without whose newspaper research it would have been impossible to trace Mary Neal's activities. It is his dedication to searching out reports and interviews from publications all over the country that has enabled Mary's voice to come across as strongly as it does.

Huge thanks are also due to Jan and Linda Pethick for allowing access to the Pethick family letter collection, and to Lucy Neal for making Mary's papers available online and at the Cecil Sharp Library to enable the story of Mary and Emmeline's extraordinary friendship to be told. She has never been less than generous with her thoughts and discoveries.

Many thanks also to the custodians of archive collections who allowed access to their collections and assisted in locating material: Frank Pemberton of Dorking Labour Party, Adam Green at Trinity College Cambridge, Harriet Costelloe at Royal Holloway archives and the teams at the English Folk Dance and Song Society's Vaughan Williams Memorial Library and the Women's Library archives.

Irene Cockcroft, Dr Lucy-Ella Rose of Surrey University, Professor Emerita June Purvis of Portsmouth University and Dr Jane Grant have provided valuable opportunities to discuss the role and significance of Emmeline Pethick-Lawrence.

I am very grateful to all who have provided images and granted permission to reproduce them, in particular the family of Alice Hawkins, the Master and Fellows of Trinity College Cambridge, The People's History Museum, Manchester, Dorking Museum, the British Library, Royal Holloway, University of London, the Library of Congress and the Women's Library, London School of Economics.

Finally, I must thank my family – Richard, Kate and Ulysses Fedrick – who have had to endure the writing process.

Introduction

At the beginning of the twentieth century, Morris dancing had died out in much of England, only surviving in pockets of the countryside. Whilst traditional folk songs had received considerable attention from collectors fearful that the nation's musical heritage would be lost, dances had not seen the same interest. In many parts of the country, the Morris was unknown and where it survived its practitioners tended to be elderly. When dancers passed on, their dances died with them. It was a suffragette campaigner and her troupe of working-class girls from the slums of St Pancras who rediscovered the Morris, revived it and brought it to new audiences, kick-starting the English folk dance revival. As a result of their commitment to preserve and pass on the dances of the past, the Morris survived as a living tradition that is performed on high streets and village greens across the country to this day.

Mary Neal was a lifelong radical, a socialist and campaigner for the rights of women and children. With her friend Emmeline Pethick, she ran an influential and experimental girls' club, the Esperance, in one of London's most deprived areas. She was also a member of Mrs Pankhurst's militant Women's Social and Political Union, the most notorious of the groups campaigning for the vote for women in the early twentieth century. Both Mary and Emmeline sat on the organisation's national organising committee. Dance and radical activism might seem strange bed-fellows but the women's embrace of traditional dance was rooted in Mary Neal's aspirations for equality and her commitment to social and political reform. She saw the Morris not as a historical museum-piece but as an activity with the potential to produce real change. And this brought her into conflict with those who favoured continuity and the status quo in cultural as well as political life.

The beginning of the dance revival and the launch of the militant campaign for the vote in London coincided almost exactly. Launched by a rather forlorn band of rebels, the militant campaign grew into a movement capable of inspiring loyalty and loathing in equal measure. The Morris revival developed from a Christmas entertainment in a club for impoverished girls into a nationwide initiative. Developing in step, both movements gathered followers from all walks of life and were closely linked. Mary's associates in the dance revival ranged from the young girls who worked in the militant campaign's offices to hunger-striking daughters of the aristocracy. *Votes for Women* magazine devoted full pages to the revival and the dancers performed at suffrage events.

This book traces the story of the indomitable and irrepressible Mary Neal and her suffragette collaborators in the Morris revival: Lady Constance Lytton, Ethel Sharp, Mabel Tuke, Emmeline Pethick-Lawrence, Laurence Housman, Lady Isabel Margesson and the young women of the Esperance Club. Mary and Emmeline provided the leadership and commitment that enabled two radical movements to flourish in the early years of the twentieth century but both found themselves marginalised after policy disagreements led to devastating splits in their respective organisations. In one case, it is the familiar story of a woman's contribution being overlooked and forgotten, the credit for her achievements going to a male rival; in the other, a willingness to put the cause above personal reputation.

The radicalism of Mary Neal's associates and of her aspirations for the dancers and for society was largely responsible for her being sidelined from the Morris revival in later years. Her teaching methods were abandoned and her contribution was forgotten for decades. It is a sad irony that, as a result, until relatively recently women were excluded from performing the very dances that their predecessors had rescued and revived as part of their campaign to play a greater part in society.

A note on terminology

The women's suffrage movement is generally regarded as having come into being in the late 1860s when the first petition demanding the vote for women was presented to Parliament. Its supporters were known as suffragists. Frustrated that after forty years of peaceful campaigning no progress had been made, Emmeline Pankhurst launched her militant Women's Social and Political Union in Manchester in 1903. Its motto was 'Deeds not Words'. The WSPU's strategy was not to persuade government to grant the vote to women, but to coerce it into doing so. The *Daily Mail* coined the term 'suffragette' to refer to the new grouping. The term was derogatory, suggesting a younger, more irresponsible, sillier sisterhood than the established 'constitutional' campaigners. But many militants embraced the term, as did the public. Non-militant campaigners distanced themselves from it. More recently, the term has come to be used for suffrage campaigners of all types, but it is used here specifically to refer to the militant campaign to which Mary Neal and those involved in the Esperance Club dance revival belonged.

Chapter One

'Sister Mary' and 'Sister Emmie' 1860–1895

Clara Sophia Neal was born on 5 June 1860 in Edgbaston, then a village on the outskirts of Birmingham. The city was one of Victorian Britain's great manufacturing centres and the Neal family was part of its prosperous business community. Clara's father was in the button-manufacturing business. Before the advent of zip and Velcro fastenings, buttons were required for every item of clothing in every household. Birmingham was the centre of the trade. Turning out everything from expensive silver, shell and mother-of-pearl buttons to cheap wooden, horn or bone pieces in its factories and workshops, Birmingham's button-makers employed 8,000 people in the late nineteenth century – many of them women and children.

The trade provided a comfortable life for the Neal family and Clara grew up at 21 Noel Road in Edgbaston with live-in servants, carriages and liveried coachmen. Like many of the city's manufacturing families, the Neals were non-conformists; Clara's parents, David Neal and Sarah Anne Smith, had married at the Mount Zion Chapel in Graham Street. David was 26 years old when his first child was born; his wife 27. A son, Arthur, was born the following year and another, Theodore, followed when Clara was 5. The Neals enjoyed an active social life and often holidayed at the seaside, journeying by train from Birmingham to North Wales. Clara loved the sea but loathed the compulsory daily ducking from the wooden bathing machines.

Handsome and well dressed, with long blonde hair, Sarah Neal was an accomplished dancer who loved parties. With her blue eyes and fair hair, Clara took after her mother. But she was nicknamed 'Miss Touch-me-not' for her resistance to being made a fuss off by elderly members of the family and her childhood was not a particularly happy one. She had a troubled relationship with her mother; Clara considered Sarah distant, preoccupied with her social life, and indifferent to the needs of her children. Though the ideal of the strong family was central to Victorian social structures, and the mother was regarded as the spiritual heart of the family, in Clara's middle-class family, as in many others, the children saw little of their parents. They were cared for by nursemaids and saw their parents for an hour or so before bedtime. Clara grew to fear nights when her parents went out to dinner, leaving the children in the care of neglectful maids. Decades later, her autobiography was suffused with long-held resentment at her parents' failure to meet the emotional needs of their children. Victorian social mores, Clara came to believe, were about appearances. 'We valued, more than anything, money, our social position, the good opinion of relatives and neighbours, an unbroken façade of family devotion no matter what the reality.'

In this conventional, outwardly happy family home, where the feelings of children were accorded little attention, the young Clara often cried herself to sleep. Eventually, her parents consulted a doctor. The 'melancholia' with which she was diagnosed, and with which she struggled all her life, would probably today be described as depression. Clara believed her distress stemmed from her parents' emotional neglect. Disappointment and distress turned to anger at the powerlessness of her position as a child. But in order to maintain the fiction of the happy home, all outward signs of childish rebellion must be suppressed, all negative feelings denied. Thwarted anger turned to despondency. The adult 'Mary' Neal believed that the pain of the neglected child had bred her independent spirit, her rebelliousness fed by fury at the hypocrisy of the appearance of the perfect family her parents presented in society but which masked what she felt to be selfishness and indifference. Her lifelong friend Emmeline Pethick expressed similar frustrations. Both ascribed their heightened desire for justice and concern for the needs of those in positions of powerlessness to the injustices and distress of their own childhoods.

But if Clara was acutely aware of her own distress, she also had a pronounced capacity for empathy, even as a child. Plagued with migraines, she learned that one of the maids suffered the same affliction, but whereas Clara was cosseted and put to bed, the maid was required to work, no matter what her suffering. Her discomfort at such unfairness was at the root of her questioning of the established order of things: why should some have to labour while others did not, and why must the family servants survive on pitiful wages (though the Neals prided themselves on being good employers) while her mother wore diamonds? In later years, she came to feel that her family's middle-class life was a pageant of snobbery where people's worth was judged on whether they had their own carriages and the number of horses they kept to pull them.

Clara had a vivid imagination and suffered from night fears, seeing wolves in the shadows on her bedroom wall. She was disdainful of her mother's shows of performative religiosity – wheeling out the maids to say prayers when a passing minister came to stay – but she had a very real belief in God. And her God was not a comforting, benevolent one: she could not bear to see the sky at night from her bedroom or carriage window for fear of seeing the very real presence of God on a stormy cloud, looking down on the world and ready to punish its human inhabitants.

Clara's schooling was eccentric and erratic in a way that was not unusual for women at the time. Her brother Theodore attended the prestigious King Edward's High School, but there was no such option for girls. Clara was removed from the local 'dame school' when she developed an unacceptable accent, learned little from the subsequent governess and was cold and hungry at her boarding school for the daughters of gentlemen in Malvern, where one of the teachers subjected her charges to such educational oddities as electro-biology, hypnotism and spiritualism (before being quietly removed for partaking of drink and drugs). After a period at home, she was only sent back to school when a cousin persuaded her mother that she was so uneducated as to be incapable of addressing an envelope. Her next school, run by two highly educated sisters, was more rigorous. The girls were expected to sit the University of Cambridge local examinations which had been open to girls only since 1867. Clara passed the examination of the College of Preceptors, the primary qualification for teachers, with a distinction in English.

By the time Clara was 20 her father had retired, though still only in his mid-forties. The family was now living at 174 York Road and Clara's 19-year-old brother was working at an apprenticeship. At 15 her younger brother was already working as a clerk. The Neal boys were making their way in the world but Clara had no employment outside the home. The expectation of a girl of her class was that she would remain at home until she married. Few trades or professions were open to women, fewer still were considered suitable for a middle-class girl, and if women who did not need to do so went out to work they were accused of taking bread from the mouths of men who needed work to feed their families. If she did not marry, Clara might expect to spend the rest of her life caring for the needs of her aging parents or acting as unpaid nursemaid to her brothers' children.

From her room in the nursery, Clara watched with envy as her brothers went work, while she sewed, arranged flowers, learned to supervise the cook, and did a little light housework (for anything more taxing would be done by the maids). Though she enjoyed dancing, whist parties, walking in the Black Country and boating, the life of an unmarried young woman was fraught with social anxiety. A girl's good name was paramount and even taking a walk alone with a young man might ruin her reputation. Sex was quite unmentionable – she got into trouble for simply mentioning glow-worms in male company for the unintended reference to the creatures' habit of lighting up at breeding time.

Reading gave the young Clara a glimpse of the possibilities of another life. She read Olive Schreiner's *The Story of an African Farm*, regarded as one of the first 'feminist' novels, though her mother was warned of its likely pernicious influence on her daughter. Henry David Thoreau's *Walden*, with its declaration of personal independence, social experimentation and voyage of spiritual discovery, all played out in a simple, natural setting, made a big impact, as did the writings of the utopian socialist thinker Edward Carpenter, with his advocacy of a freer and more just society. (Both Schreiner and Carpenter later became friends.) John Stuart Mill's *The Subjection of Women*', arguing in favour of legal and social equality between men and women, increased Clara's discontent with her lot as a woman, though what she thought as a young woman of his promotion of the cause of votes for women is not known.

In 1883, Andrew Mearns published 'The Bitter Cry of Outcast London'. This sensational pamphlet revealed to middle-class readers the appallingly squalid conditions endured by the poor of Britain's urban slums. It engendered feelings of horror, anger and sympathy in many of those who, like Clara, subsequently dedicated their lives to social reform. Her middle-class complacency shattered by the revelations in 'The Bitter Cry', Clara determined to volunteer her services to alleviate some of the suffering catalogued in the book. Her natural empathy, and her sense of resentment at the injustices in her own life, may have motivated her decision to leave the family home to work with the urban poor, but her non-conformist religious background surely also played a part in her desire to make a difference. The powerful Birmingham non-conformist community was politically and socially engaged and at the forefront of the visionary social reforms in the 1880s that saw the city become something of a model for urban redevelopment. Clara's family had been Baptists for generations. Joseph Chamberlain, Birmingham's reforming Liberal mayor, a Unitarian, was a fellow non-conformist. His radical use of public money to fund civic improvements for the benefit of its inhabitants transformed the city. His reforms provided clean water, gas supplies, parks, schools and libraries. Slums were cleared to create wide, ventilated thoroughfares and healthy housing. Death rates for the city's inhabitants fell dramatically. But the situation in London, the heart of Queen Victoria's empire, remained appalling. Work for many was irregular, casual and badly paid. Male unemployment was high and many households relied on sweated female labour. Rising populations had led to overcrowding and squalor. By the 1880s, conditions in London's slums had given rise to anxiety amongst the middle and ruling classes about the threat of disease, moral depravity and public disorder on their doorsteps.

In 1888, at the age of 28 and still unmarried, Clara Neal left the family home and journeyed to London in search of a purpose for her latent talents. She applied to join the West London Methodist Mission in Cleveland Street as a 'sister'. Missions and settlements brought together volunteers from higher social classes to live together in small communities in close proximity to impoverished neighbourhoods. Members went out to study the living conditions of the poor at first hand. Their purpose was not to transform society but to understand the poor and to alleviate the worst suffering. Many middle-class women like Clara offered themselves up for service in organisations like the West London Methodist Mission.

The lives of the working classes were regarded as something of an exotic mystery and working with a mission offered women something of the freedom and excitement of their male counterparts who were going out to the colonies to study and convert native peoples to Christianity. Impoverished urban neighbourhoods were often depicted in print as another country where things were different; London was even referred to as a 'dark continent', inhabited by wild races, and poor Londoners were described as heathens, 'English Kaffirs', 'street Arabs' or 'Hottentots'. Such terms made it clear to readers that the poor were not like 'us'. They were to be pitied – and feared. But, it was believed, middle-class women could be their salvation, offering education in moral values and bringing people to God. In Victorian society, self-sacrifice was promoted as a female virtue and giving up family life and comfortable homes to do such work appealed to spiritual young women like Clara who took up their roles with missionary zeal.

The West London Mission was newly founded by the Welsh Methodist orator Hugh Price Hughes. His wife, Katherine, led a group of female social work volunteers, known as sisters, who went out into the community to work with disadvantaged families. The girls were of good families; one of Mary's fellow sisters was Lady Katherine Thynne, daughter of the Marquess of Bath. (She later married Evelyn Baring, 1st Earl of Cromer and leader of the Men's League for Opposing Women's Suffrage.) Missions provided a surrogate family structure that was reassuring to parents; Clara would live at the Mission House at 10 Fitzroy Square, just south of Regent's Park, with other staff and volunteers, under the watchful eye of the founder and his wife. Clara seems to have drawn a line under her previous life and reinvented herself; like a nun casting off her old identity, she took a new name. Clara Sophia became 'Sister Mary'.

At the age of 10, Mary had dedicated her life to Christ and through him to helping those less fortunate than herself; in pledging herself to the Mission she was able to make good on that promise in a practical manner. Mission work neatly fulfilled Victorian ideals of womanly service. Rather than clamouring for the vote or for an education, questioning the social order or trying to break into the professions, through the missions a young woman might turn her energies and spirituality to helping those in need, whilst safely asking no questions about what order God might have ordained, and why those lower down the social scale might be in need of the ministrations of a young girl with experience of nothing very much.

Mary arrived in at Euston station on a cold February day in 1888, a tall, thin young woman with vivid blue eyes and light brown, curly hair. The change from her life in Birmingham was profound. Where she had enjoyed a spacious family home and a room of her own, here there was just a cubicle and a crowd of new sisters. She was unused to the constant noise, the lack of privacy and the cold. And what she found in the London slums was profoundly shocking. On her first night at the Mission Hall, she observed a congregation of the filthy and despairing being encouraged to give up their sins and come to God; the enormity of what she had chosen to do filled her with despair.

With virtually nothing by way of training, the Mission sisters were sent out to visit families, often crammed into one single room in once-grand houses, in order to assess their needs and whether the Mission might help them. The filth, pest infestations, and lack of sanitary arrangements appalled Mary; often she had to hold her throat to prevent herself retching at the stench. In these lives she could see not a glimmer of hope. It took all her determination that first winter not to give in to despondency and return to the comforts of home. With little idea of what could be done to improve the lives of those who lived out their time in the slums, her main objective was to encourage them to attend services at the Mission Hall.

In the England of the 1880s, there were no old-age pensions, no widows' pensions, no unemployment benefits, and no compensation for accidents sustained at work. The only 'safety-net' for those unable to work, and for their dependent families, was the threat of the workhouse. The squalor, depravity and despair she saw during her years at the Mission, and the understanding she gained of the people she met – particularly women and girls – coloured Mary's thinking for the rest of her life. In her campaigning work she prided herself on not having an academic understanding of poverty, but a practical one that led her to seek practical solutions.

Though work at the Mission was hard, Mary found the freedom she had been looking for, 'working,' as a lifelong friend later put it, 'as a free person in a community of equals'. As with all the sisters, she was required to take her turn in charge of the Mission's girls' club which met several evenings a week at Cleveland Hall. This she found to be an unruly place of dubious benefit to the factory girls who attended. Club nights were riotous, with dead cats lobbed in through the windows and furniture thrown about. It was decided that continuity of leadership might bring some sort of order, with just one sister in permanent charge. Mary was selected as the one best able to cope with the behaviour of the girls. Her practical good sense, fearlessness, plain speaking and sense of humour came into their own in this role. On taking charge, she turned the girls out, allowed just four in, and told them that four more would be admitted on following nights only when the original four had proved their ability to behave; she increased the numbers by four each night.

The girls Mary met through the Mission could not have been further removed from those of her experience – garishly dressed, with a fondness for large hats, they swore freely and many were sexually active. They were defiant of authority and sometimes violent, destroying Mission property and fighting. But as she got to know them, Mary came to respect the young women as individuals. She wrote in her autobiography:

No words can express the passionate longing which I have to bring some of the beautiful things in life within easy reach of the girls who earn their living by the sweat of their brow. If these clubs are up to the ideal which we have in view, they will be living schools of working women, who will be instrumental in the near future, in altering the conditions of the class they represent.

Her task was to improve the girls' life experiences, not simply as an end in itself but as a means of affecting the way the young women went on to bring up their families. The belief that middle-class women could 'improve' working-class women, and thereby improve society generally, was a commonly held by mission workers of the time. Clubs were designed to widen the girls' horizons and to offer opportunities for enrichment, but they also provided an improving environment aimed at developing the moral character of their members.

In particular, concern about the sexual morality of poor young women motivated many who ran girls' clubs. In Victorian society, women were expected to act as moral guardians for men who were excused an inability or unwillingness to control their sexual impulses. Ideally, girls should be chaste and chaperoned – things that slum girls often were not. Many were working from a young age and had a physical freedom that middle-class girls did not. They were therefore considered to be more vulnerable to falling into 'temptation' or leading young men from the path of chaste living. To counter these risks, it was the role of middle-class club leaders to police the young women's behaviour and to offer firm moral guidance. Through exposure to 'lady-like' role models, instruction in the domestic arts, and contact with 'refined' recreations, it was hoped that clubs would improve girls' expectations and shape them into compliant and feminine mothers who would raise thrifty, religious, chaste and respectable families.

The moral failings of slum women were considered to be the result of delinquent parenting – rather than of financial and physical circumstances beyond their control – compounded by their lack of status within their own communities and families. It was the duty of women like Mary to lead those less privileged than themselves to blossom into respectable womanhood. Sexual activity, bad language and physical exuberance were discouraged in an attempt to make slum girls more like demure middle-class girls. Girls who had spent all day in cramped factory conditions were therefore taught to calm down, rather than encouraged to take up sport or other physical activities. Neatness and punctuality were encouraged, as were improving activities – sewing, cooking, singing and drill. Wholesome entertainments were considered more suitable than the dance halls, pubs and music halls that the girls were used to. Singing and drill were thought to develop self-control, discipline and cooperation; dancing was not encouraged as it was considered likely to degenerate into unseemly 'rowdiness'.

Mary had been at the Mission for three years when she made the most significant friendship of her life. In 1891, a young woman named Emmeline Pethick arrived to join the sisters and was assigned to assist Mary in running the girls' club. The relationship with the Mission and its founders would not last, but that with 'Sister Emmie' would sustain them both through extraordinary endeavours and personal trials, from prison, through war and into old age.

Emmeline Pethick came from a similar stratum of society to Mary: comfortable but not establishment. Both young women had grown up in middle-class, mercantile families in the provinces; neither had been educated to any profession and both found themselves in their twenties looking for a purpose in life. They both seem to have had extraordinary reserves of energy and determination and had been drawn to leave the comfort of their families to find their way in the metropolis at the heart of the Victorian empire.

Emmeline was seven years younger than Mary. Born on 21 October 1867 in Bristol, she was the first surviving child of thirteen, only seven of whom survived childhood. Her father owned a tannery in Bristol and imported hides from South America. In 1876, the family moved from a modest house in Bristol to a large house in Weston-super-Mare. The Pethicks employed a live-in cook, two housemaids and a children's maid, and kept a coachman/groom at the lodge next door. Like Mary's, Emmeline's parents were, for the most part, distant and the children inhabited their own nursery world, cared for by nursemaids who did not much care for them or for the work. Emmeline likened the nursery to a prison, 'We were in the hands of those who possessed delegated authority over us, and from that authority there was no appeal.' The fight against injustice was to become one of the guiding principles of her life.

Emmeline was sent to a 'ladies' boarding school where, at the age of 8, she learned that to cry in homesickness in front of the servants was to demean herself. Like many thoughtful children, she felt misunderstood, and her anger at perceived injustices may have fuelled her passion for justice and the desire for change in later life. The Pethick family was also non-conformist. Born a Methodist, Emmeline's father had abandoned formal religion and rejected the idea of a vengeful God. He was forward-thinking on social matters, buying his daughters bicycles at a time when many considered such a thing unsuitable for respectable ladies. Of the five Pethick girls, only one took the conventional path of marriage and motherhood. Emmeline's sisters supported her when she joined Mrs Pankhurst's radical campaign for the vote, though their mother rather regretted that they were 'not like ordinary girls' but 'rather too forward'.

Mary was immediately struck by the charismatic newcomer with the slight gap in her front teeth and head of dark, unruly hair. Years later, she recalled Emmeline's beautiful eyes and dignified, attractive voice. The younger woman had been 'finished' at a local establishment for young ladies, where she learned that having an opinion was 'unladylike', and had then travelled to France, where she had failed to learn much French, and to Germany, where she became fluent in the language. And then, as Mary had done, she had returned home to her parents' house to wait for whatever husband fate might bring her.

There were seventeen years between Emmeline and her youngest sibling. With her schooling over she was expected to help her mother in the care of her young brothers until such time as she was married. Soon her sisters joined her at home. Perplexed at the prospect of sex and sexuality, she seems to have concluded with relief that she was not the type of girl who was likely to attract a husband. Like Mary, she wanted to find her own way and at home she was restless, irritated at her dependence on her father. The maids, it seemed to her, had more autonomy than she did, able to throw in their jobs and move employers, whilst young women like herself, with no means of earning money, must conform to their fathers' mores and strictures into adulthood. In offering her services to the West London Mission, 23-year-old Emmeline Pethick was motivated as much to achieve independence for herself as to make a difference in the world. She found an immediate soulmate in Mary Neal.

Like Mary before her, Emmeline entered the Mission with a somewhat naïve belief in the ability of a young woman with no experience of anything except middle-class life to make a difference to the lives of the struggling London poor. The Rev. Mark Guy Pearse recommended her to Mary as an assistant. She was, he told Mary, 'an idealist and very sensitive and wouldn't believe anyone was unhelpable'. She would get a shock, he warned, but she would hold on to her belief. Shortly after Emmeline's arrival in London, Mary was taken ill with suspected tuberculosis. She was not expected to survive. (Her brother Arthur later died of the disease.) She was sent to recuperate with her parents who by now had moved to Bournemouth. This presented a problem for the Mission. Mary had already asked if the new recruit might be assigned to assist her; now she hastily showed Emmeline around the Mission Club and left Sister Emmie to cope as best she could.

That first evening, Emmeline set out for Cleveland Hall alone in a state of trepidation but she managed to control the girls by playing games with them that she had played with her younger brothers. Like Mary, Emmeline found herself well suited to youth work. She was not put off by hardship, she loved children and brought a sense of fun to her work. Mary was not away long. Frustrated at her parents' house, she told her doctor that she would rather work a week in London than spend twenty years in a bath chair in Bournemouth. After her somewhat surprising recovery she and Emmeline ran the club together. The two women quickly came to operate as partners and became firm friends – equals in energy, determination and vision. Thereafter, Mary supported Emmeline in everything she did like an attentive older sister; when Emmeline was forcibly fed fifteen years later, Mary claimed to feel the pain.

Mary and Emmeline made a formidable and complementary team. Where Emmeline was romantic, emotional and sentimental, fond of quoting the Bible and myths, Mary pretended to be incapable of sentiment and prided herself on her practicality and sharp tongue. She joked to Emmeline that she had a heart like a dried-up piece of leather. Her devotion to the girls suggested that this was quite untrue, and she was able to see the fantastic side of things and to delight in it. Where Emmeline inspired devotion and collected passionate followers throughout her life, Mary tended to provoke either violent like or dislike. But she cared little about being liked and more about getting things done. Unlike Emmeline's myriad intense friendships, Mary was selective about who she spent her time with and had a small circle of intimate friends. But, recalled Emmeline, she had no malice towards anyone.

The sisters worked in the Mission dispensary and creche, went out to visit the sick and the dying, and put on entertainments for the elderly inmates of the workhouse. In the overcrowded and squalid slums around Euston, they came across all manner of social distress – from drunkenness and prostitution to incest and extreme domestic violence. Conventional advocates of thrift, hard work and temperance, they were committed to improving the moral character of the daughters of the urban poor. But, over time, a waning of their conventional Christian faith was accompanied by ambition for social change as they came to understand more of the precarious lives of the girls and their families. The realisation that, despite working long days in the clothing trade, the girls they worked with were unable to make enough money to live on, whilst the profits of their labours supported the middle-class daughters of business owners like themselves, led to a questioning of the whole economic system. 'It seemed to us,' wrote Emmeline in her autobiography, 'that the world was upside down, and being young we felt very hot about it, and had perhaps half unconsciously an idea that we and the enlightened young people of our day could do something to set it the right way up.' The poverty and social deprivation the pair encountered in the London slums had led them to socialism. In time it would also lead them to the fight for the vote, not least because even charity discriminated against women. No help, for instance, would be given to wives deserted by their husbands, no matter how dire their circumstances, lest giving assistance to such women should lead men to conclude that they could abandon their financial responsibilities without fear that their children would be forcibly separated from their mothers in the workhouse.

Mary's first writings for the Mission Report were unexceptional pieces about the joy brought into hard lives by the Mission sisters, but over the years her writing became more political. In 1893, she supported the West Yorkshire miners' strike, raising money for strikers and writing pieces about 'The Coal War' for the *Methodist Times*. When a group of miners' wives came down to London from Castleford, she took charge of the party, stayed with them in rooms at Smithfield Market, and assisted in the arrangement of demonstrations and street-corner collections to raise money for the strikers' families. When she accompanied the women home to Yorkshire, she received a huge welcome and went out to speak in local chapels. The following day, she was taken down a mine, an experience which affected her deeply. What she learned of the hardships of the lives of the miners and their families seems to have further radicalised her. In response to accusations in the press that miners lived in luxury and ate smoked salmon, she refuted the ridiculous suggestion, but also asked why a man who toiled for ten hours a day in the dark should not eat smoked salmon when a man who lounged all day in a West End club was not criticised for doing so. The strike, she wrote, was part of the struggle between the privileged and the working classes, between labour and capital, a struggle with which she now allied herself.

Although her involvement in the miners' cause was not discouraged by the Mission leaders, Mary's growing commitment to social change took her well beyond her remit as a sister. With her growing radicalism came misgivings about the aims of the Mission and doubts about its limited aspirations. She and Emmeline began to question the purpose of the Mission, organising a conference on what the response of such clubs should be to such industrial questions of the day as impacted on the welfare of working girls. Sister Mary had also come to question whether coming to God would do much for the condition of the working poor. 'For five years we spent every morning interviewing hopeless down and outs, and I doubt if we ever did any permanent good to anyone,' she reflected later. She also asked whether teaching girls a more middle-class standard of conduct was not 'a bitter mockery' until their living conditions were improved by better housing, wages and hours of work.

Many years later, Mary recalled that the living and working conditions of working people that she experienced during her time with the Mission had brought her to the conclusion that charity and philanthropic work were futile. It made, she said, no dent in the 'hard crust of poverty and degradation in which so many of my fellow creatures lived'. In fact, initiatives like the Mission that alleviated the worst effects of endemic poverty might actually be making the situation worse in preventing working people from taking action to improve their lot. 'Much social work was really keeping people from realising their position and keeping would-be helpers from making efforts to bring about a better state of things,' she later wrote. She and Emmeline, she concluded, were colluding in keeping things as they were. 'I woke up to the realisation of the need for political and economic changes which would not be mere palliatives, but which would make such radical changes in conditions.' By 1895, she had come to question the very purpose of the Mission to which she had devoted herself.

Unusually intelligent, resourceful and determined women who had discovered their capabilities, Neal and Pethick were also frustrated by the constraints the Mission placed on their freedom to experiment. They wanted to introduce the girls to dance and drama, neither of which were encouraged by the Mission. In involving themselves with the wider movement for social change they had outgrown the role of the Mission. Reading a new life of St Francis of Assisi by M. Sabatier, both were inspired by the saint's embrace of poverty. The Mission household, they concluded, with its maids and servants, was too middle class and comfortable, insulated from any real understanding of the lives of the poor. The household's servants and regular meals isolated the volunteers from those with whom they worked. Fired with enthusiasm for their new vision, Mary and Emmeline tried to persuade the elders of the Mission of the necessity of living a simpler life amongst those that they wished to help. But the Mission leaders, Mary felt, were too orthodox, too conventional and too timid to consider a different way of doing things. Their request to live amongst the people they served was refused. If Mary and Emmeline wanted to experiment in the hope of really making a difference, they would have to go it alone.

Perhaps another reason for the women's departure from the Mission was a waning in their missionary enthusiasm for bringing unbelievers to the faith. On one occasion, Mary commented that working girls needed material help more than they needed Christ. Organised worship seems to have played little part in the later lives of either woman, nor does a Christian god feature prominently in their writing after this period. Their spiritual beliefs seem to have become more mystical: Mary recalled crossing a meadow one evening and the world becoming luminous from a hidden source of light. 'Unreality vanished into reality and an incredible happiness filled my consciousness,' she said. She claimed that the feeling of union with every living thing that she experienced never left her. Such spiritual feelings may have been what drove both Mary and Emmeline, but they were not obviously Christian. Their religion seems to have evolved into a mix of undefined spirituality and socialism. One of the last events organised by Mary and Emmeline at the West London Mission was a great May Day pageant, with children dressed in white dancing around a pagan maypole which now symbolised, Emmeline reported, the 'international holiday of the Sons of Labour'.

Both women had grown in confidence in their time with the Mission. Mary had developed her writing skills; Emmeline had discovered the calling as a public speaker that was to serve her so well in the women's suffrage movement. They had spent the formative years of their adult lives at the Mission; the decision to leave was not an easy one, but in the late summer of 1895 the pair handed in their resignations. They went to Emmeline's parental home in Weston-super-Mare to plan their new venture. Not only would they establish their own organisation, allowing them the freedom to pursue their own initiatives, they would also, for the first time in their lives, live fully independently.

Chapter Two

'Dreaming the Impossible Dream': The Esperance Girls' Club 1895–1905

On a November day in 1895, Mary Neal and Emmeline Pethick left the comforts of Weston-super-Mare. They arrived at Paddington station in late afternoon with no home to go to, no reassuring organisation to support them nor comrades to welcome them back. They had little money and no experience of living independently. 'We put our large trunks in the cloak-room,' Mary later recalled, 'just like the servants come up to look for work.' Taking the bus to Canning Town, they were welcomed at the settlement there by Percy Alden who had offered them temporary lodgings. For the first time they would live neither with biological nor Mission 'family'. Mary was 35, Emmeline 27. Many middle-class Victorian women never left the family home unless they married but lived in the care and under the supervision of fathers and brothers their whole lives. Mary and Emmeline were not totally free of parental influence, however, as both relied, to an extent, on family income to support themselves.

As part of a move to fully share the lives of those with whom they would work, they took a small flat in a block designated for working men at 20 Somerset Terrace, off Duke's Road, behind St Pancras church in Euston. It was not far from their old friends at the Mission. They learned how to live on £80 a year, paying a rent of 14s 6d a week and each putting £1 a week into their housekeeping fund. Emmeline had a small allowance; Mary would write to earn money. Conditions were very different from the Mission House at Fitzroy Square. Much of Somerstown was classified by Charles Booth in his survey of the streets of London during these years as housing those in casual work and chronic want, with whole streets housing the lowest class of 'vicious' and 'semi-criminal' elements. Conditions were verminous and insanitary. The winter of 1895 was hard. Standpipes in the road supplied water to frozen households and Mary and Emmeline had to keep soup and hot coffee available to warm those who came to them for help. Households faced unemployment, hunger and sickness, lacking even coal or warm clothing. So endemic was the problem of poverty in the metropolis that they might quite reasonably have given up all hope of making a difference. But, Mary recalled years later, they had 'dreamed the impossible dream' of a better world. Though that dream might often seem hopeless, they told themselves that it was only those who dared to dream for whom the dream might become reality.

Both Mary and Emmeline recalled their time at Somerset Terrace as one of personal happiness, freedom and new-found agency. They learned to cook for themselves, cultivated a wide circle of like-minded, progressive friends and lived a life of purposeful activity. Mary revelled in the fact that she wrote her magazine columns on politics and social issues (under an assumed male name) with one hand stirring the cooking pot. The visitors to Somerset Terrace were an eclectic mix. Old ladies from the workhouse came regularly to take tea by the fire on their day 'out'. Radical thinkers, politicians and campaigners like Edward Carpenter and Havelock Ellis sat in front of the same fire. The women formed bonds with the leaders of the Labour movement; Labour Party leader, Keir Hardie MP and future Labour leader, George Lansbury were visitors. Mary respected Hardie's principles, ideals and strength of character, and credited him with bringing her into the movement. He later professed himself delighted by the Morris revival, understanding the appeal of beauty to those living in squalid conditions.

The women's commitment to socialism was the driving force in their lives. Emmeline explained that it was 'in her bones', describing her inspiration in characteristically quasi-religious terms. Her commitment, she said, stemmed from her 'clearest, strongest and most inveterate sense of the dignity and worth of the human body and soul above everything else,' which had forced her 'into a life-long campaign – against every sort of bondage, against all sorts of established authorities: and it … has kept me (not by choice but by inward necessity) always against the stream.' She had framed her life as a prolonged crusade, in partnership with Mary.

Obtaining the vote for women did not figure strongly in their priorities at this period. Another regular visitor to Somerset Terrace was future Labour Prime Minister James Ramsay MacDonald and his wife, Margaret MacDonald née Gladstone. Like Emmeline and Mary, Margaret had come to socialism through voluntary work in youth clubs, though in her case with boys. She had also studied political economy under the leader of the National Union of Women's Suffrage

Societies (NUWSS), Millicent Fawcett, and she sat on the organisation's executive committee. So it is likely that the question of women's suffrage was discussed at Somerset Terrace. Emmeline wrote in her autobiography that her first reaction to hearing about the campaign for the vote for women was puzzlement, 'It dawned on me that some women cared tremendously, cared to the point of recklessness. I asked myself why?' For she and Mary had put their faith in socialism to end injustice.

It soon became clear that their own flat could not accommodate their ambitions. In 1895, they established their own girls' club. Funded by a small group of local benefactors, none of them very well-to-do, they raised the 8 shillings necessary to rent two rooms at 45 Grafton Street. Initially opening for two hours nightly, the aim of the Esperance Girls' Club was to improve the lives and opportunities of the young women who toiled in the sweatshops of the West End clothing trade. In this sense, its objectives were not very different to those of the Mission's girls' club. The girls might escape the drudgery of work and home for a short time, playing games, singing, dancing, sewing, cooking, visiting galleries, listening to lectures and talks – all activities through which they might develop socially, intellectually and spiritually. But the club's ambitions widened in terms of what it would offer and the range of age demographic that it would serve. Emmeline became the club's musical director, introducing the girls to music that was otherwise outside the realm of their experience. In the summer, older girls asked for half a crown to make lemonade for younger siblings and in the autumn they asked if these younger siblings, left playing in the street, might be brought inside. Many of the children's parents worked long hours in the sewing trade and of necessity the children were neglected. Always open to new opportunities, Mary initiated a dedicated play space for younger children. The girls were now doing the leading, showing Mary and Emmeline their needs and identifying solutions and the Esperance became a seedbed of social experimentation.

The two women had concluded that the degradation of slum lives was less a consequence of poor moral standards and lack of aspiration and more of structural issues such as urbanisation, industrialisation and capitalist economics. Unjust laws and exploitative employment practices were compounded by patriarchal attitudes to women. Women were not to blame for the lack of decent housing or for poor working conditions. From their original desire to 'improve' the girls by encouraging them to adopt middle–class values, they had come to question the whole capitalist system. Unlike trades unionists or more conventional club workers, Mary and Emmeline did not see the women's morality and working conditions as separate issues but as interlinked. They came to understand, rather than to judge, the behaviour of girls who were overworked and poorly paid, not properly fed or clothed and who often shared one room with their parents and siblings. They came to appreciate the temptations of prostitution or payment for sex by masters of the houses where the girls worked, and to believe that the moral character of the girls was not the issue but rather that the fact that neither the culture nor the law offered any protection to vulnerable young women whose physical work and family circumstances put them at the mercy of predatory men. Lack of work for much of the year was more of a driver of prostitution than promiscuity, and patriarchal family structures offered no protection to girls from the actions of fathers or brothers or from entitled employers. They came to understand the mindsets of young women who knew that all that stood between starvation for their families was their needle or scrubbing brush. In a pamphlet, Mary pointed out that women who lived on the edge of destitution were often judged by middle-class standards as irrational, immoral, or hysterical without any understanding of the realities of their situations. The more she and Emmeline learned of the lives of the girls, the more appalled they were at the degradation of women in the home and in the workplace and by the lack of protection offered by the law or by society generally.

Their hours at the club undoubtedly cheered the lives of many of its members but Mary and Emmeline had concluded that offering temporary relief from hardship and turning out rounded and self-controlled young wives was not enough. The young women that the club served were generally employed in the fashion business. They worked long hours in the social season but they had no job security and only sporadic work out of season which meant that they could not adequately clothe and feed themselves throughout the year. Prostitution in the 'off' season was an economic necessity for many. And at home they suffered emotional, physical and sexual abuse, hunger and lack of sleep in vermin- and bug-infested tenements. As Mary put it in her autobiography:

We never lost the overwhelming sense of injustice and wickedness of a social system which drained the workers of youth and vitality to fill the pockets of employers and capitalists and it was the havoc made amongst the young girls that especially filled us with the determination to do something practical to alter the state of things. One after another we saw the children who formed our Junior Club leave school for the most part healthy, alert, rosy-cheeked, to become in a couple years anaemic, tired, listless.

Two hours of recreation at the club after ten or twelve in hot workrooms, she concluded, was not enough to make any real difference to the girls' health or well-being.

Lives must be changed, the pair concluded, not simply made bearable and socially acceptable. They advocated a move away from pure charity and towards political action as an aim for such organisations as the Esperance. As Emmeline put it in an article in 1909, she and Mary had discarded the idea of philanthropy in order to pursue fairness. The club developed a political as well as a philanthropic mission. Infringements of the factory and workshop acts, of which the pair became aware through talking to the girls, were reported to the authorities. Important politicians were invited to visit. A citizenship class was established to discuss housing and social and political issues and the girls were introduced to the idea of political action and to the concept of trades unions with whom they might work to improve their conditions. 'We had ... to give them a conscious part to take in the battle that is being fought for the workers and will not be won until it is loyally fought by them as well,' she wrote in 1898. Well before they became involved in the campaign for the vote, Mary and Emmeline had begun advocating for women's social and political organisation, bringing hope and instilling courage so that the girls might play a part in the struggle to transform society.

They were criticised by socialists for wasting their time in seeking to extend to a handful of youngsters the benefits that the capitalist economic order had bestowed on their own class, rather than throwing their energies into attempts to change the system to the benefit of the working class generally. In order to address some of these issues, in December 1896 Mary announced to the London *Evening Standard* that she and Emmeline would set up a dressmaking cooperative. In order to find new ways of facilitating social change, they proposed to conduct an experiment to see if such a business, run on equitable terms for the workers, was viable.

The business would have to compete with the employment models of London's fashion houses. Girls employed in dressmaking workshops customarily worked seventy to eighty hours a week completing orders in the run up to the summer season, labouring in unventilated rooms with no time off for rest or food. In the low season they were laid off without wages. This employment model, of intense labour for part of the year and little work for the rest, ensured maximum flexibility for employers. For the employees it meant much of the year with little or no income; they could not afford decent living accommodation, recreation, or medical treatment, nor make provision for times of sickness, unemployment or old age. Mary and Emmeline calculated that the girls' living conditions could be improved if the profits generated by the sale of expensive suits and gowns were to be distributed, not to business owners and shareholders, but amongst the women producing them.

Launching a fashion house was a risk, especially for two women who had never run a business. But, Mary told the *Evening Standard*, it was better to fail than to sit and lament while their sisters sweated to death or worse (by which she surely meant prostitution). She estimated that it would take £100 to set up a small workshop. Neither she nor Emmeline had access to funds, so they launched the fundraising initiative with £10 that had been donated to the Esperance Club.

Maison Esperance was launched in August 1897 at 80 Wigmore Street. It paid its female employees at least 15 shillings a week, which the women had calculated to be the minimum required to maintain a decent standard of living. It guaranteed regular work for eight hours a day, throughout the year, in well-ventilated rooms, offered annual leave and did not demand overtime in the season. Young women working for Maison Esperance were freed from the fear of destitution during the winter slack period and from the drudgery of the long spring days working day and night completing outfits for the summer season.

Mary and Emmeline approached the business in a professional manner, recruiting experienced workers and a manageress from Paris. The experience they gained served them well in their future initiatives. With fixed hours, the business did not have the flexibility of workshops which enforced long hours of overtime; this meant turning away business in the season and covering wage costs in winter when there was little work. The business would not have succeeded without the support of socially aware customers. The pair called in favours from friends and family and sought to tap into the social consciences of public-spirited wealthy women via pieces in supportive newspapers. Women such as such as Countess Brownlow and Alys Pearsall Smith, Bertrand Russell's first wife, were concerned about working conditions of those who produced their gowns, and willing to support a business with an ethical profit-sharing model.

The improvement in the girls' quality of life was immediately apparent. But Maison Esperance was just one workshop amongst many hundreds and Mary, now with practical experience in the industry, campaigned against the conditions of 'sweated' workers generally. She spoke at conferences, wrote articles and made recommendations for regulation and changes to working practices. In a pamphlet on dressmaking written in 1906, she described the drudgery and bitterness of anaemic girls who had never been outside on a June day and who could only hope as the years passed that the time might come when 'a sane, wholesome and beautiful life will not be impossible to anyone who contributes to the wealth of the community'. She and Emmeline were by now embedded in the Labour movement. Keen to share their understanding of the social and economic realities of women's working lives, they hosted a cooperative conference at 155 Great Portland Street in December 1897. In 1899, Mary spoke in Ealing and attended the London International Congress of Women; the following year she and Emmeline attended a convention of trades unionists, radical clubs, peace unions, prison reform associations and educational charities. In December 1900, Mary campaigned on behalf of the progressive candidate in the local elections. By 1903, she was being invited to speak across the country.

Not all the Esperance Club's activities were overtly political or economically motivated, however. In her youth, Mary had spent time walking in the Black Country, and Emmeline was a keen explorer of the countryside surrounding London which was accessible from Somerset Terrace by rail. The pair would describe their excursions to the girls, most of whom had never left the city. In June 1898, they took the girls of Maison Esperance on the first of what were to become annual 'beanfeasts' to Pinner. These trips were followed by an Esperance Club holiday to Bisley in Gloucestershire. Recalling this first holiday, Mary regarded the sight of the girls singing at night in a pine wood, free from the sordidness of their surroundings, as vindication of their dreaming the impossible dream. But she also recalled the anxiety of the girls in unfamiliar surroundings, concluding that they had been disinherited, and had lost the security of the earth beneath their feet, mystical conclusions which later played into her attempts to reclaim country dance for town girls exiled from their country origins.

The club returned to Bisley the following year, then took trips to Surrey where they rented cottages in a hamlet at the foot of Leith Hill. The girls saved all year to contribute their 10 shillings towards the costs of the accommodation and Mary and Emmeline had to obtain written confirmation from every employer that the girls would not be dismissed for their week's absence (for which they were, of course, not paid). After several years holidaying in the countryside, they ventured to the seaside at Littlehampton. They were in the vanguard of a movement that would eventually see the development of holiday camps for working people and the establishment of the youth hostel movement. In April 1900, they announced to the press a proposal to buy a seaside hostel for working youngsters. As they had when founding Maison Esperance, they called for funders. Mary wrote a booklet entitled 'Dear Mother Earth' and sold shares in the operation for a penny. She wanted, she said, for every girls' club to have a summer holiday and proposed to put her years of experience in Gloucestershire, Surrey and the seaside to use, advising on catering, housekeeping, boat chartering and train journeys. The hostel would be simply furnished and let at rates calculated to cover the expenses of running the building rather than at a profit. She and Emmeline joined forces with Lily Montagu, who with her sister, Marion, ran a similar club to the Esperance, the West Central Club for Jewish girls.

When not in use by the Esperance or the West Central, the house by the sea in Littlehampton was rented by clubs of all denominations for working people and children. Mary and Emmeline named it the Green Lady after the myth of Demeter and her daughter, Persephone, reflecting their faith in the power of the pure air of the countryside to rejuvenate modern urban woman. Mary described Emmeline as a mystic, but a practical one, neatly summarising their vision at this time:

> If living in close touch with the unseen forces and in touch with the beautifying vivifying forces of earth and sky and sea and a power to transmute these life-giving spiritual forces into the sternest practical work is not being a mystic then [the term] would have no meaning for me.

She later recalled girls who had no experience of anything outside their London streets thinking barley fields were shrimps ready for picking, and that all lanes were mews. The girls and children revelled in singing folk songs, of living without errands and without constant rules. When old women were allowed use of the hostel, and married women with their children, they were surprised to find that they were allowed to come and go as they pleased, rather than being subject to the rules of others. The catering at the Green Lady, recalled Lily Montagu, could be curious and unsatisfying, the windows inadequate, the mattresses soft and the crockery chipped, but 'no house in the world could ever have entertained happier groups of girls and women'.

Mary and Emmeline's belief in the restorative powers of the countryside reflected a nostalgia for the perceived purity of the pre-industrial past. This was summed up in a playlet performed in 1908 by the Esperance girls. Written by Alfred Sayers, (who became the auditor of Mrs Pankhurst's Women's Social and Political Union), it tells the mystical tale of a town girl going to the country where she is awakened and her heart set singing. It neatly sums Mary and Emmeline's view of town folk as disinherited from the earth that is their birthright. These strands of thought fed into many of the Esperance's activities, but none more so than the dancing for which the girls would soon become famous.

Busy with the club, Maison Esperance, club trips and their writing and speaking engagements, Mary and Emmeline looked set for a lifetime working together. But in 1900, the unexpected happened. At an age at which women were considered to have been left behind in the marriage market, Emmeline Pethick met an unusual young man. At 29, Frederick William Lawrence (1871–1961) was four years younger than she was, Eton and Cambridge educated and independently wealthy. Trained as a barrister but with no need to work for a living, he spent his time travelling the world and giving free legal advice to those in need. He was the voluntary treasurer of the Mansfield House University Mission in Canning Town. In early 1900, Mary and Emmeline attended an event at the Mission with the Esperance girls. It was discovered that no arrangements had been made to provide tea for the visitors; hastily, the treasurer went out to purchase provisions. Mary claimed to have predicted that same evening that Fred (as he was known) was the man that her friend would marry. However, Emmeline initially turned down his proposal on the grounds that her duties as a wife would be incompatible with her campaigning activities and of her objection to his plan to stand as a Liberal Unionist candidate at the next Parliamentary election, which she, as a socialist, could not support. The couple also disagreed over the morality of the second Boer War being promoted by the Liberal Party and which she regarded as no more than a campaign of murder for profit. The couple separated. Fred travelled to South Africa to observe the treatment of the Boers. When he returned he offered his services to relief efforts for Boer women and children and embraced socialism. In May 1901, Emmeline accepted his second proposal.

On 2 October 1901, Emmeline Pethick married Fred Lawrence at Canning Town Hall. Slum-dwelling club girls mixed with members of Parliament at an unconventional ceremony organised by Mary Neal and held during the midday dinner hour to enable working guests to attend. Fred's MP uncles made it a condition of attendance that they should not have to mix with David Lloyd George, who, like Fred, had opposed the Boer War. Fishermen came from Littlehampton and the bathing girl from the beach there. One guest stole a teaspoon only to return it to Mary a week later. Fred later recalled that he had married his wife because she smoked, could get off a moving bus, and went out walking without gloves. Respectful of her desire to keep her own identity, he added her name to his.

Mary put a brave face on it and, when asked how she felt, claimed not to have lost a sister but to have gained a brother. But the marriage brought huge change to her personal life. Until now, the two friends had worked and lived together. Emmeline now left the modest rooms that they had shared for a grander life as the wife of a wealthy man, with a serviced apartment next to the Royal Courts of Justice on the Strand, and a country home in Surrey. Fred invested in and began to edit a left-leaning newspaper, *The Echo*. On their first wedding anniversary, he demonstrated his belief in his wife's independence by giving her the keys to a separate flat for her own use. Even he was not to have a key.

Mary continued to live at Somerset Terrace. She spent some time in Wales, covering the bitter Penrhyn Quarrymen's strike for *The Echo* and carried on running the Esperance. Herbert McIlwaine (1858–1916) took Emmeline's place as the club's musical director. Born in Belfast, McIlwaine had worked as a horse-breeder and journalist in Australia before returning to London where he published a volume of short stories based upon his experiences in Australia. He was living at the Passmore Edwards Settlement, where it is likely he met Fred Pethick-Lawrence, who introduced him to Mary. He was to become Mary's chief collaborator in the Morris revival.

Emmeline had no intention of retiring to live the life of a wealthy lady. Money had given her opportunities. She and Fred loved to travel and she was often absent from the Esperance Club for months at a time, but her new home in Holmwood, a few miles south of the Surrey town of Dorking, became a weekend retreat for her extended 'family'. Two large loft rooms in the house were converted into makeshift dormitories for Mary and the Esperance girls. In 1904, she and Fred bought and demolished a couple of cottages just north of their country home and built a holiday home specifically for their use. Named 'The Sundial', the cottage was designed by Arnold Dunbar Smith, who had designed the Passmore Edwards Settlement Centre where Mary had set up the Esperance's first dedicated children's play centre. The Sundial still stands at the roadside in Holmwood, its mural and cheerful inscription facing out on to the common: 'Let others tell of storm and showers, I tell of sunny morning hours.'

Emmeline and Fred divided their time between Surrey and their political and philanthropic activities in London. *The Echo* was not a success and when it ceased publication Fred took on the *Labour Record and Review*. Emmeline regularly contributed articles – in her uplifting spiritual style – to its 'Page About Women'. Rather than circumscribing her activities, marriage brought her new opportunities as Fred supported her in her determination to share the good fortune of their wealth. She and Mary looked set to continue in a purposeful round of club holidays and campaigning. But in 1905 they found their paths beginning to widen and diverge. Both of their trajectories would have a huge impact on the Esperance girls, seeing them drawn into the public and political arena.

Chapter Three

Mary and the Morris; Emmeline and the Suffragettes 1906–1907

In July 1905, Herbert McIlwaine read about the activities of Cecil Sharp (1862–1933) in the *Morning Post*. Sharp was a music teacher who had collected and published a volume of folk songs. The performance of folk music and dance was in decline in many areas of the countryside by the early twentieth century and the urban girls of the Esperance would have been more familiar with the songs of the music hall than those of their rural ancestors. The loss of this musical heritage was a matter of concern to Sharp and other collectors who made it their business to ensure that the songs of the countryside did not lapse into obscurity. Over the previous two years, he had been collecting songs from elderly singers in rural villages, recording their words and tunes, and was regarded as something of an authority. He believed that such songs were a link to the nation's 'natural' music and made efforts to collect them from folk who were 'untainted' by exposure to education and modern music.

There was growing nostalgia at the beginning of the twentieth century for aspects of the past that had been lost to industrialisation and the movement of working people to the cities over the previous 100 years. This manifested itself in a revived appreciation for rural traditions. Much of the impulse was romantic; towns and cities were smoggy, filthy, vermin- and crime-ridden and overcrowded; the past, and the countryside, offered an alternative, pre-lapsarian vision even if it was agricultural poverty that had driven many workers to the cities in search of reliable wages. The interest in folk music from such collectors as Cecil Sharp was part of a wider impetus to regain what was seen as a simpler and more wholesome way of life that had been lost. For many, the countryside represented more than just a relief from the crowding of the city; it symbolised an alternative vision for society. Followers of John Ruskin and William Morris rejected the mechanisation and industrialisation of mass production, which they felt had deprived humanity of its dignity. Lucy Broadwood, a member of the piano-manufacturing family and a near neighbour of Emmeline's in Capel near Dorking, had been collecting folk songs since the 1890s. Her family friend Ralph Vaughan Williams was also in the vanguard of efforts to preserve folk traditions, taking notation of traditional songs from Surrey gamekeepers and labourers. He was, he said, motivated by the chance of 'picking up some rare old ballad or an exquisitely beautiful melody,' which might be, he said, 'worthy, within its smaller compass, of a place beside the finest compositions of the greatest composers.'

Mary's involvement in the dance revival seems to have come at a time of some disillusionment. Her mood at the end of the Esperance Club's annual summer holiday in July 1905 was one of despondency. Contemplating the sun, sea and freedom of the girls' two weeks in Sussex and knowing the dark, dank homes and the long hours in workshops to which they must return, she had begun to doubt her ability to achieve any real change:

> I was tired of the few hours in which we vainly tried to lighten burdens far too heavy for young shoulders to bear. I was tired of interviewing employees, sitting on Committees, soliciting charity, and the coming winter looked very dark and very hopeless. I longed for some life-giving wind which would sweeten those lives and lessen the weariness, some weapon which would conquer the dirt and the dreariness and the muddle in which these city girls lived.

After nearly twenty years of social activism, she was ready for a change of direction. While they were waiting to return to London, Herbert McIlwaine suggested that her girls might learn some of the traditional songs that Cecil Sharp had collected from 'unlettered folk' in the countryside. Mary then went to meet Sharp at the Hampstead Conservatoire where his tenure as principal was coming to an end. Like Mary, he was disillusioned with his professional life, and open to new ideas and opportunities. The meeting would be a turning point in both their lives.

Sharp was a member of the Fabian Society and a man of moderately progressive views. He was more than happy to supply songs to Mary's girls. His desire to reclaim the nation's lost musical heritage resonated with her efforts to reconnect the city girls of the Esperance with elements of national culture from which they had been deprived by the circumstances of their lives. He prophesised, she later recalled, 'by a spiritual sixth sense', that they would reclaim their lost inheritance in song. Probably unaware of Mary's driving commitment to bringing about social change in the most unlikely of ways, Sharp sent her away with a copy of his 'Somerset Folk Songs'. 'It was as if the club had gone mad,' Mary later recalled about the first singing session, 'they were perfectly intoxicated with the music.' Sharp was quickly invited to see the girls perform the first songs they had learned: *Seeds of Love*, *Lord Rendal*, *Blow Away the Morning Dew* and *Mowing the Barley*.

In the autumn of 1905, Mary went back to Sharp to ask if he might know of any traditional dances. She and Emmeline had already encouraged the girls in physical activity in the form of drill and callisthenics. The physical degradation of the Britain's urban underclass, largely the result of poor diet and adverse working and housing conditions, was a cause of concern to politicians, commentators and social campaigners alike at the turn of the nineteenth and twentieth centuries. The nation based its right to rule over half the world on the supposed superior character and strength of the Anglo-Saxon race; the poor physical specimens of Britain's own cities was a national embarrassment which potentially undermined the country's assumed right to rule. Drives to improve the fitness of the working classes had seen drill introduced in schools, and gymnastics had become a staple activity of church and youth clubs. In May 1905, the Esperance girls had performed gymnastic exercises with other girls' clubs to a crowded audience at the Queen's Hall, London's main concert venue. On presenting an award to the Esperance girls, Lady

Aberdeen, president of the Women's Industrial Council, had announced that she wished that everyone who felt anxious about the deterioration of the race might have seen the display and congratulated the girls on learning 'self-mastery'. Emmeline was quoted in the press promoting the effect of these competitions in fostering healthiness, organisation and cooperation amongst the girls. Dance might be expected to encourage the same virtues.

But Sharp had no dances to offer. Instead, he sent Mary to William Kimber of the Headington Quarrymen Morris dancers in Oxford. Sharp had come across the bricklayer playing the concertina in 1899 and had recorded some of the tunes he played but not the dances that they would have accompanied. The Headington men had passed their dances down from father to son for generations (though not without a break, after which the company was revived). There were no published manuals or dance teachers; if the girls were to dance to the beat of their ancestors, they would need to be taught by its rural practitioners. In October, Mary took a train to Oxford and a hansom cab to Headington. There she persuaded Kimber and a cousin, Richard, to come to London to demonstrate the dances to the girls.

Herbert McIlwaine met the Oxford men at the station. On their arrival in London, they taught three sessions which were received with great enthusiasm. 'The result of their coming far outran our fondest anticipations,' Mary recalled in the first *Esperance Book of Morris*:

The Morris, like the magic beanstalk, seemed to outsit the law of nature: we saw it in the heart of London

rise up from its long sleep before our very eyes … The
first dance that was set before these Londoners … was
Bean Setting. It represents the setting of the seed in
springtime. Of course, the music, its lilt and the steps
that their forefathers had footed to it in the olden
times, were as little known to these, the London born,
as the ceremonial of old Peru. As little known, yet not
strange at all; it was a summons never heard until now,
yet instantly obeyed: because, though unfamiliar and
unforeseen, it was of England, and came, even though
it was centuries upon the way, to kinsfolk.

Within half an hour of the arrival of the Headington men,
Mary claimed, 'Bean Setting', in all its intricacy with clashing
staves, was in full swing in London. The instructors were
allegedly both amazed and delighted. In addition to 'Bean
Setting', they also learned 'Blue-eyed Stranger, 'Constant
Billy' and 'Shepherd's Hey' that night.

The response when the girls sang and danced for an
audience of 200 at the club's Christmas party in December
at the Passmore Edwards Settlement Hall was rapturous.
The audience of well-to-do benefactors and supporters
was described by McIlwaine as representing 'literally every
element in contemporary society'. Keir Hardie was there, as
was Laurence Housman, the writer, artist and activist who
would go on to found the Suffrage Atelier in support of votes
for women. Housman told Mary that she must not keep such a
national treasure 'in the narrow area of a girls' club'. She must
show it to the nation.

Emmeline said that there was something in the rhythm of folk music that found a response in Mary's heart. With her belief in the spiritual connection between humankind and the earth, she saw the dance as mystically linked to an older, kinder and more equitable society. The purification and restoration of working people through contact with the natural world had always been a feature of her vision; now the dances of the past became inextricably linked to her aspirations for the future. She wrote in her autobiography:

> And that night there awoke, after generations of sleep, a little stir of an older life, an older rhythm, an older force, in tune with a simpler life, a sweeter music ... [with] vibrations ... and rhythms of an older world, a world untouched by machinery and mechanized power but responsive to the vibrant rhythm of sea and wind, earth and stone.

In April 1906, the Esperance dancers gave their first ever public performance, combining song and dance at the Queen's Hall. The *Daily Telegraph* explained to readers that though the young women knew no musical notation, they learned quickly by ear. The journalist's words are very probably quotations from Mary:

> When it is recollected that all the singers were born in the heart of London, that few of them have any kind of knowledge of country life, it is the more to be wondered at that songs breathing the very air of the land should go so straight to the hearts of these

girls that they will have nothing else. An indefinable something in the music itself found its response … and the greater ease with which they learn the genuine folk song seems to show that the national music is inherent in their bones.

It is not hard to imagine the excitement of girls who would have shared between them a smart dress or a hat feather, now costumed in what *The Scotsman* described as 'quaint old-world country dresses' – muslin gowns, bonnets and flowers – for a paying public. Before the performances, Cecil Sharp gave an enthusiastic lecture, predicting the future of folk music to be with the urban poor: 'I prophesize that within the year the slums of London and other large cities will be flooded with beautiful melodies, before which the raucous, unlovely and vulgarizing music hall song will flee the night mist before the rays of the morning sun.' Until now his interest had been in song, but the reaction of the public to the Esperance dancers opened his mind to the possibilities of dance. Like Mary, he saw the culture of the past as a liberation from that of the present. His belief in the potential of folk music to 'civilise' the urban masses coincided with Mary's desire to restore the lost heritage of her girls. But the dancers were not presenting the dances exactly as they would have been seen 100 years earlier in at least one crucial respect. Traditionally such dances would have been performed by men, so these first steps in the Morris dance revival were already radical. It was city girls who would give back to the nation dances that historically their sex would never have danced.

The Queen's Hall event raised £55 for the Esperance Club's holiday fund. That might have been the end of the matter had it not been covered in the national papers. *The Scotsman* declared the performances as 'a striking demonstration of what can be done with a little enthusiasm to spread a knowledge of the old English folk songs and Morris dances, which still linger in the country districts'. In the following weeks and months, invitations for the girls to dance came in from around the country. With her skills as an organiser and publicist, Mary took full advantage of this opportunity. She and the girls began to travel the country by train, bus and cab. They were invited into the cottages of country folk and to the mansions and stately homes of the wealthy. They performed in schools, training colleges and factories. Undoubtedly the girls were a novelty; witnesses expressed surprise at the contrast between songs of 'sweet and simple England' and singers from 'this grimy latter-day London' singing of morning dew when they had never seen a dewdrop. It was often the first time that hosts had mixed socially with girls from the lower orders, and Mary recalled that it was often a revelation to them. One reporter found it hard to believe that the girls were 'working lasses from Cumberland Market' and 'real cockneys', so enthusiastically did they throw themselves into country songs, dances and games. In their way, the girls were educating the better classes out of their prejudices about what young urban women were and what they were capable of.

Mary came to believe that their enthusiastic receptions signified something more than simple appreciation for a novelty well executed; she saw public reaction to the dance as representing a deep and instinctive connection with something primitive and life-giving to which people responded without understanding why. 'Everywhere these boys and girls ... welcome these songs and dances as if some ancestral meaning, some instinctual knowledge recognised them and loved them,' she wrote.

Demonstrations and teaching engagements had to be fitted around the girls' work and initially Mary travelled with them. In a very short time, the girls of the St Pancras slums had come to be regarded as 'experts', their skills recognised and valued. The Esperance girls were claiming a place for themselves in a society that had written them off. In November 1906, more than thirty girls danced in Maidenhead to raise money for the town working men's club. Once a charitable cause itself, the club was now raising money for others. Something of the simply joyous atmosphere can be gleaned from the local newspaper:

The whole performance was given in Old English costume, dances and songs alternatively. It was pure English jollity and prettiness from start to finish, and the only matter for regret was that the entertainment did not last half an hour longer, since at the end of the ninety minutes the delighted audience were yearning for more.

By end of the year, the Esperance dancers had sent teachers to Somerset, Devon, Derbyshire, Monmouth, Norfolk, Surrey and London.

Lady Isabel Margesson was one of the first well-to-do women to take an interest in the dance. She invited Mary, Cecil Sharp and Herbert McIlwaine to Foxlydiate House in Worcestershire and introduced them to the Bidford dancers whom she had invited to Redditch to train local people to perform in a pageant. Sharp and McIlwaine transcribed several dances including 'Bluff King Hal' and 'Morris Off' from the Bidford side. Following this visit, one of Mary's girls, Florence 'Florrie' Warren, was invited back to teach local people. Mary and Lady Isabel would soon cross paths again for the dance was not the only new initiative in which Mary had now involved herself. Lady Isabel was a committed suffrage supporter. A member of her local branch of the National Union of Women's Suffrage Societies, she was on the point of joining Emmeline Pankhurst's more radical Women's Social and Political Union (WSPU). Quite possibly she was recruited by Mary who found herself drafted into the campaign for the vote just as her new venture in dance was taking off.

As Mary rehearsed the Esperance dancers for their first public performances in early 1906, Emmeline had taken her first steps towards the leadership of the militant campaign for the vote for women. Though they were advocates for women's issues, and had carved out independent lives for themselves, until 1906 neither Mary nor Emmeline had had much involvement in the campaign. But they had come to the realisation that if women's poverty and suffering was ever to be relieved then women must have a voice in the government of their nation. This realisation was to have a profound effect on their lives, and on the lives of many of the dancers and some of their benefactors alike. Recalling her work with the Esperance and on councils and committees, Emmeline related that she and Mary had been 'appalled by the tide of human misery that swept past our door'. They had come to believe that the law was unfair to the poor and to women and to the realisation that they could do little for:

> [T]hese ill-paid girls, these deserted and ill-used and overworked wives, these 'sweated' widows, struggling to fulfil the duties of both parents! – never could we, who as women knew them and understood their needs as no men could understand them, never could we or any women come to their rescue.

In articles justifying her later actions, Emmeline recounted memories of a little girl sent mad in fear of the workhouse, and of the suicide of an exhausted girl of 20. In a piece written in 1909 she recorded the haunting effect of those two cries: '[they] still ring out at times in my memory with their terrible indictment against life as men have made it. They have led me, those voices and other voices, they have called me on to where I am now, in prison.' But though the two may have concluded that the legal and social systems framed by men did not serve the needs of women, neither seems to have involved herself with the suffrage campaign before 1906. Perhaps they had attended meetings of local suffrage societies – in her autobiography Emmeline claimed frustration that her local society had been helpless, resigned and anxious not to make a fuss. 'I felt the need of women's enfranchisement.

I passionately desired it for the sake of a better humanity. But I did not see the way to get it,' she wrote.

By 1900, women had been campaigning peacefully for the vote – via letters, articles, meetings with MPs and petitions to Parliament – for thirty-five years. In 1903, an exasperated Emmeline Pankhurst had formed her militant organisation, the Women's Social and Political Union (WSPU), with its motto of 'Deeds not Words', in Manchester. Rather than trying to persuade parliamentarians that women deserved the vote, she intended to force the government into action. In October 1905, as the Esperance girls were learning their first dance steps, Mrs Pankhurst's eldest daughter, Christabel, and a mill girl named Annie Kenney had taken what is regarded as the first militant action. They deliberately got themselves arrested at a meeting at the Free Trade Hall in Manchester. This forced the issue into the headlines and into the national debate. Emmeline Pethick-Lawrence was travelling in South Africa at the time but Mary, running the Esperance with McIlwaine, found her interest piqued. She proposed to write a piece about the action for Fred Pethick-Lawrence's *Labour Record and Review* and when Emmeline returned home she drew the incident to her friend's attention.

Emmeline expressed interest and early the following year Keir Hardie introduced her to Annie Kenney and Mrs Pankhurst's middle daughter, Sylvia. Mrs Pankhurst had concluded that the WSPU needed a base close to Parliament and to the national press; Sylvia and Annie had been tasked with establishing the organisation in London. They had few resources, the one training as an artist, the other a semi-educated mill girl. Nor did they have experience of managing money, which was in any event scarce, but they did have contacts – the leader of the Independent Labour Party being one of them. Emmeline was not initially convinced by Hardie's proposal that she should become treasurer to the WSPU's fledgling London office. She had to be talked into taking the role. Although she supported the cause in general, she and Mary had put their faith in socialism to end injustice and she feared that involvement with a single-issue organisation would divert her from seeking wider social change. It was only on meeting Mrs Pankhurst that she was convinced that socialism delivered by men would do little to change the lot of women and that she should quit campaigning for the Labour Party and devote her time to campaigning specifically for the vote for women. The WSPU supported no political party (since no party had unequivocally committed itself to introducing a bill to give the vote to women) and required its members to devote themselves to the one cause. As she took a role in the organisation's leadership, Emmeline must have been convinced that securing the vote for women should take priority over the achievement of more general socialist policies. But if she was convinced of the cause, she was not initially convinced of the effectiveness of Mrs Pankhurst's little band of warriors. 'To tell the truth,' she later recalled, 'I had no fancy to be drawn into a small group of brave and reckless and quite helpless people who were prepared to dash themselves against the oldest tradition of human civilization.' In retrospect, she framed her recruitment with a semi-religious sense of destiny:

It was not without some dismay that it was borne in upon me that somebody had to come to the rescue of this brave little group and that the finger of fate pointed at me. What is become of my friends and what to become of my country home I do not know [she told Mary], for this is going to take all my time and interest.

Mary accompanied her friend to the first formal meeting of the London office of the WSPU at the home of Sylvia Pankhurst's landlady in Chelsea. There she met Sylvia, Mrs Pankhurst's sister Mary Clarke, and Nellie Martel. With her customary practicality she took the notes of that historic first meeting. She must have been convinced, both of the cause and of the ability of the group to shake up the women's suffrage campaign, as by the end of the meeting she had joined the London organising committee alongside Emmeline. She stressed the necessity of the inexperienced group engaging a qualified accountant and recommended the services of the Esperance's accountant, Alfred Sayer. 'I am the proudest man in London because you asked me to help this glorious work, when you had not a penny and were down at the bottom,' he later told her. One of Mary's first donations came from the playwright George Bernard Shaw. She was already heavily involved with the Esperance Club and with Maison Esperance. Now she was in the inner circle of the very active WSPU, soon to be patronisingly dubbed the 'suffragettes' by the *Daily Mail*. The dance revival began to take off almost simultaneously.

The WSPU had managed to recruit two organised, resourceful and well-connected women. Emmeline played a key organisational role in establishing the campaign in London, paying off the organisation's debts, raising money and directing policy. The apartment that she shared with her husband at Clement's Inn, next to the Royal Courts of Justice, became the organisation's London office. As treasurer, Emmeline was responsible for fundraising, for the establishment of a chain of regional offices and for the recruitment and employment of paid organisers across the country. She and her husband provided the WSPU's practical business foundation as well as contributing significant amounts of their personal wealth to the cause. Together they launched and edited *Votes for Women* magazine, which allowed the organisation to communicate with members all over the country, and which would go on to sell 50,000 copies a week. But she was more than an effective director of finance; she brought gaiety and spectacle to the WSPU with her interest in dance, drama and pageantry. She understood the appeal of symbolism and colour and introduced a celebratory style which promoted women's achievements and introduced the organisation's distinctive colour scheme of purple, white and green. And she brought with her followers with time and energy to devote to the campaign; very soon Mary and Emmeline were joined on the London committee by Mabel Tuke, who was already volunteering with the Esperance girls. Mabel would fulfil the role of secretary until the outbreak of the First World War.

Without the Pethick-Lawrences it is doubtful that the organisation would have expanded at the rate that it did on its move to London. 'It was a great day when Mrs Pethick-Lawrence joined,' recalled Christabel. Her mother told a court in 1912 that the situation had been dire when Emmeline was persuaded to take control of the organisation's finances. 'Providence sent the right woman at the right time to help in turning the tiny vessel into a great liner,' wrote Annie Kenney in her autobiography.

In the autumn of 1906, as Mary toured the country with the Esperance dancers, Christabel Pankhurst came to London; she would live with Fred and Emmeline at their Clement's Inn apartment for five years. With her mother away touring the country, it was Christabel, together with Emmeline and Fred, who formulated much of the WSPU's policy and tactics and ran the day-to-day business of a large national organisation. Peaceful marches aimed to persuade government of the strength of support for the cause, but women were arrested if they tried to speak in the environs of Parliament. Great hopes had been aroused by the Liberal Party's landslide election victory in January 1906 when many candidates had expressed support for women's enfranchisement. The Labour movement was expected to support the Liberals to bring in legislation. There was huge disappointment when no proposals were forthcoming and Prime Minister Campbell Bannerman refused to give any assurances. Christabel now advocated giving up trying to convert MPs to the cause, since their loyalties were to their parties. Instead they would attack the party system itself, campaigning against candidates of the governing Liberal party at by-elections (whatever their personal views on women's suffrage), in the hope that if the government lost seats as a result of its failure to grant the vote to women it would capitulate and bring in the necessary legislation.

On 23 October 1906, Emmeline was arrested for the first time for trying to make a speech outside the Houses of Parliament. She and her companions refused to give an undertaking to keep the peace since to do so would have amounted to an undertaking not to campaign. Nor would they pay the fines imposed on account of their refusal. She was sent to Holloway for two months. According to the papers, the scene in the courtroom was almost 'indescribable' when the sentences were announced as banners were unfurled and the women shouted as they were dragged defiantly from the dock. Prison was a traumatic experience. 'My heart died within me,' wrote Emmeline, recalling the claustrophobia of the prison van, 'It seemed to me that I was in my grave, forgotten by the world.' She suffered something of a breakdown. Fred begged Mrs Pankhurst to be allowed to pay Emmeline's fine in order to secure her release. She was forced into a humiliating undertaking to keep the peace and released into Mary's care. Mary later recalled that Emmeline was so changed by the experience of prison – haggard, dazed and dishevelled – that she would never have known her.

While Emmeline recuperated with Sylvia Pankhurst in Italy, Mary ran her establishments in London and Surrey and Fred stood in as the WSPU's treasurer. Mary was deeply affected by her friend's imprisonment. On dining with a friend who disapproved of their actions in pursuit of the vote she experienced the odd feeling of Emmeline having taken possession of her and found herself mimicking Emmeline's gestures as she justified herself. The feeling lasted thirty-six hours, during which time she went down to Surrey and wrapped herself in one of Emmeline's coats. It was nearly three years before Emmeline braved prison again.

The actions of Emmeline and her comrades in going to prison inspired many women to take up the cause. One such was Evelyn Sharp. Cecil Sharp's youngest sister was an ambitious and talented woman who had left the family home to establish herself as a writer in London. In October 1906, she was reporting for the *Manchester Guardian* on the conference of the National Union of Women Workers, when she heard Elizabeth Robins, a fellow committee member of Mary and Emmeline at the WSPU, speak. Evelyn Sharp's skills as a speaker, journalist and editor would make her one of the WSPU's greatest assets and bring her firmly into Mary and Emmeline's orbit. Her mother was very concerned about her taking any sort of militant action that might risk prison, however, and she gave a promise not to do so. Her brother, who had taken the respectable position of music tutor to the royal princes, was less than pleased with his sister's new associates.

While Mary juggled management of the Esperance and the dancers' engagements with looking after Emmeline's domestic arrangements and her commitments to the WSPU, Sharp was turning his attention to the dance. He had published a book of songs; now he worked closely with Mary, McIlwaine and the Esperance girls to put together a collection of dances. He took musical notation while McIlwaine transcribed the steps learned from the traditional dancers, as demonstrated by Florrie Warren, Mary's lead instructor. *The Morris Book* was published in April 1907. With an eye on the teaching market, it included descriptions of eleven dances that could be taught in schools. The book was dedicated to 'Our friends and pupils, the members of the Esperance Girls' Club'. Sharp acknowledged Florrie Warren's contribution and paid tribute to Mary, who, he said, 'not only made the venture possible in the beginning, but with her power of help and organisation gave it a reach and strength that neither of us could have given'. He was publicly acknowledging that Mary had played a similar part in launching the dance revival to that of Emmeline in the WSPU.

Mary and Sharp enjoyed a strong friendship in these early years of the dance revival. She later said that these were the happiest years of her life. She and Sharp had much in common; both came from families in trade and held progressive views. The dance revival was a fulfilment of Mary's desire to enable deprived young people to develop full and fulfilled lives. She had always recognised the intelligence, curiosity and creativity of the young women whose social deprivation allowed no outlet for their talents, ambitions and dreams. In introducing the dance to the girls of the slums she was not just introducing them to a musical heritage from which they had been excluded, she was nurturing their talents – for organisation, for teaching, and for engagement beyond their social class. She was using the power of dance and song to transform lives.

Florrie Warren was a teenager when she was orphaned and taken under Emmeline's wing. She was 20 years old when she demonstrated steps for Sharp. Another of Neal's most successful dance teachers was Blanche Payling. Blanche grew up in St Pancras, and lived near Cumberland Market, the daughter of a packer. Her brother was a metal polisher and her sister an errand girl. Yet by 1911 she was able to describe herself to census enumerators as a teacher of dancing, having danced and taught all over the country. On being engaged to teach at the home of Lady Muriel Paget she found herself teaching the wife of the Home Secretary, Herbert Gladstone. She was brought breakfast in bed and took dinners with Lady Paget, attended by three liveried footmen. Mary was proud of girls like Blanche and Florrie. 'It is not a small thing for a little London dressmaker to stay in the house, as an honoured guest of a country squire,' she wrote, 'and to ride in his motor car and write letters home at his study table, and feel at the same time that she too has something to give.'

Mary had collected the first dances from the Headington Quarrymen and she continued to collect and preserve traditional dances. In later life, she recalled elderly men guiding her from the house of one dancer to another, sometimes playing the fiddle as they sat beside her chauffeur. She invited elderly dancers up to London so that they might better pass on the steps and spirit of the dances, giving them a tour of sights during their stay. There was, therefore, a strong link between the traditional dancers and the young Londoners. The importance of that direct link was one that Mary claimed made the Esperance dancers' interpretations 'authentic'. In her pamphlet 'Set to Music', published in 1907 and dedicated to Sharp, she described the challenges of collecting:

It was hard to ascribe authenticity to any particular rendition of the dance. It is not easy to describe the actual steps and figures ... for no two sides of dancers did a particular dance in precisely the same way. No two men in the side did the step in the same way, and no one danced it in exactly the same way on two separate occasions.

And there were so many variations between traditional Morris sides:

Some of the traditional performers danced with straight knees, others from other villages bend the knee; some never put the foot out at the back; others disregard this, but the traditional dancers have always plenty of spring and lightness about them.

Cecil Sharp was also now collecting dances as well as songs and with his growing expertise he began to consider making a career as 'folklorist'. But, unlike Mary, he had a family to support. If he was to give up teaching, he must find a way to monetise the folk revival, and to do that he needed to be recognised as the leading expert in the field. He continued to recommend Mary's expertise to others and to give introductory lectures to performances by the Esperance girls, but he was looking to build his own reputation in the world of dance. And the question of 'authenticity' – and who should decide what was and was not 'authentic' (and therefore acceptable practice) – would soon become a point of contention between them.

The Esperance dancers had learned their dances from traditional dancers; in turn, revival dancers all over the country had learned from them. With publication of the first Morris book, dances were being passed on second and third hand. Invitations for Mary, Sharp and the Esperance girls to dance and to teach at shows and festivals came flooding in. To those disappointed or appalled by the degradation of urban industrial life, the dances became a symbol of a pure 'Englishness' that many felt to have been lost to urbanisation. In the spring of 1907, Mary and McIlwaine were invited to take a group of girls to dance at the Shakespeare Festival in Stratford. In doing so she was taking unschooled girls who might never have seen Shakespeare to England's cultural capital and claiming a place for them there. Afterwards, Edward Burrows, inspector of schools for the Portsmouth and West Sussex area, who had been impressed by the performance of a group trained by Florrie Warren, invited Mary and McIlwaine to stay at his home in Sussex. In July, he convened a large meeting of enthusiastic trainee teachers in Chichester and Florrie was invited to teach them to dance. 'It has seemed to us this year that we have made a great discovery of a hidden treasure,' Mary recorded Burrows telling the gathering in 'Set to Music'. He urged the teachers to become a medium through which others might enjoy the dance, going out into Sussex schools, and Florrie was engaged for five weeks to teach another batch of teachers. It was the beginning of a process of formalisation of dance training that would eventually see Mary and the Esperance marginalised.

By the autumn of 1907, both the militant campaign for the vote and the Morris revival had picked up a momentum that neither Mary nor Emmeline could have predicted. The WSPU had mobilised women around the country and marches, rushes on Parliament and mass gatherings were producing copious newspaper headlines. Mary's dancers were travelling the country, gaining attention wherever they went. But in both initiatives trouble was brewing. In September 1907, Mrs Pankhurst faced a challenge to her leadership from committee members unhappy about the direction the campaign was taking, particularly the tactic of targeting candidates from the governing Liberal party. The dissenters demanded that the organisation be run in a democratic manner, with open discussion of policy and elections to executive roles. Mrs Pankhurst dismissed proposals that members should be allowed to vote on leadership positions; instead, she announced that she would retain power in a committee appointed by herself. The move split the committee, with a number of high-profile members opting to form a rival militant organisation, the Women's Freedom League. Emmeline backed Mrs Pankhurst, arguing that it made no sense to have the carefully thought-out strategy to hit the government where it hurt undermined by newcomers with little political or campaigning experience or to engage in discussions on tactics that would undermine unity and weaken the operation. Emmeline and Mabel Tuke elected to remain on the WSPU's organising London committee which became the organisation's national committee. Mrs Pankhurst asked Mary to remain on the committee in the belief that her reputation outside the campaign would inspire confidence in potential supporters. Evelyn Sharp also stayed with the WSPU.

The controversy over the direction of the women's suffrage movement might have been expected to have little impact on the activities of the dancers. But the Esperance would soon be drawn into campaigning activities and by the end of the following year the club would have provided the WSPU with one of its most influential campaigners. And the differing responses to the increasingly radical tactics employed in the campaign would fuel a dispute that was already brewing between the two main promoters or the dance revival.

The Roots of the Morris

The roots of the Morris are shrouded in mystery and much debated. It has been suggested that the dances originated in Spain to celebrate victory over the Moors and that they were introduced to the English court on John of Gaunt's marriage to Constance of Castile in the fourteenth century. If that is so, the dance's origins would have been sophisticated and courtly. Others have speculated that the dances originated in processional dances that had marked Catholic feast days until the Reformation and which were danced by Guilds on village greens. By the early twentieth century, the dances were generally only to be seen in rural villages, but this does not mean that they did not have their origins in cities or in court entertainments.

Whichever is correct, they are unlikely to have been democratic, inclusive dances that anyone might join in. Nor are they likely to have been fertility rituals going back to prehistory. Influenced by the anthropologist Sir James Frazer and his popular study of European folk culture, *The Golden Bough: A Study in Comparative Religion*, Mary Neal and Cecil Sharp both became convinced of the dance's pagan roots. They saw the Morris as containing remnants of pagan fertility rituals and pre-Christian religious ceremonies. But modern experts generally dismiss the theory as fanciful and without evidence. That they were so insistent on the primitive origins of the dance tells us more about early twentieth-century desires to root the dance in prehistory than it does about the real history of the Morris.

Experts now believe that the dances were celebrations within communities, entertainments that brought communities together, invented and reinvented by those who danced them. The Morris is generally assumed to be 'traditional', but the dances were not unchanging through the generations; they had evolved over centuries to the point at which their steps were written down by Mary Neal and Cecil Sharp and their collaborators. It is unlikely that performers from the sixteenth century would recognise the similarity with surviving photographs of mid-nineteenth century dances and dancers. All attempts to pin down 'authenticity' have achieved is a snapshot of how the dances were performed at one particular moment. Whatever its origins, the Morris has undoubtedly changed and evolved over centuries and has continued to do so since the revival.

The Morris revival has been described as more an 'invention' than a revival since the practice had all but died out across much of the country by the early twentieth century. Though they did not conceive of it that way, Mary Neal and Cecil Sharp and their collaborators can be regarded as actively 'inventing' the Morris 'tradition' as much by what they regarded as unworthy or not part of the 'tradition' as by what they chose to collect and spread across the country.

'Florrie' Warren

Florence 'Florrie' Warren (1887–?) grew up in the Somerstown area of St Pancras. Mary recalled her as a young girl, entranced by the sea on a moonlight trawler trip on a club holiday. She was a naturally gifted dancer and became Mary's most valued soloist and demonstrator. As the Esperance's lead instructor, she travelled the country performing and teaching. Cecil Sharp and Herbert McIlwaine worked with Warren on the first Esperance Morris book, taking notation from steps as she demonstrated them. Florrie's vital contribution was acknowledged and the book featured a photograph of her dressed for the dance. Mary was furious when the dedication was removed from later editions and her dancing impugned by Sharp as 'hoydenish'.

In December 1910, Florrie sailed with Mary to the US. Performing to large audiences, she was considered something of a star and asked to perform in a masque at Carnegie Hall in New York. Her performance was followed by a ball at which dancers who she had trained gave a performance. Such a reception in the cultural centre of New York was a world away from the slums of St Pancras where she had grown up.

At a tea party in honour of the English visitors in Boston, Florrie met a young lawyer named Arthur Brown. Months later she and Mary were on the liner preparing to return to England when Brown jumped aboard and proposed. Mary returned home alone. Florrie remained, accepting teaching engagements in the US. Back in England, Mary raised funds for a wedding gift from those who had appreciated Florrie's teaching. Florrie Warren and Arthur Brown were married on St Valentine's Day 1912. They went on to have three children, Cicely, Dorothy and Vida. Like her mother a dancer and gifted teacher, Vida Olinick Brown became ballet mistress for George Balanchine, travelling the world with the New York City Ballet.

Florrie returned to England with her husband for a brief visit in 1937. At a reunion of Esperance dancers, she danced with Vic Ghirardi, (brother-in-law of Fred Pethick-Lawrence's secretary Esther Knowles, herself an ex-Esperance performer), who had been a key member of the Esperance men's side.

Lady Isabel Margesson

Lady Isabel Augusta Margesson (1863–1946) was one of the first well-to-do supporters of the Morris revival. In June 1906, shortly after the Esperance girls' first public performance at the Queen's Hall, she invited Mary Neal and Cecil Sharp to meet the re-formed Bidford dancers at her home, Foxlydiate House near Redditch in Worcestershire. She had invited the Bidford men there to teach local youngsters to perform at a masque in her grounds. Sharp collected eight tunes from the Bidford side and Herbert McIlwaine took notes of the steps. Several of the dances later appeared in the first Esperance Morris book. Lady Isabel's dancers continued to dance at local events for several years.

The daughter of Lord Frederick Hobart-Hampden and titled in her own right, Lady Isabel was a woman of influence, used to mixing with aristocrats and government ministers. Her brother was the Earl of Buckinghamshire. In 1886, she had married Mortimer Margesson. She was a prominent suffrage supporter, serving as president of the Redditch Women's Suffrage Society from 1904 until her resignation to join the militant WSPU at roughly the same time as she was hosting the dancers in Redditch. It is very likely that she and Mary Neal knew one another through their existing suffrage connections, and that she was recruited into the militant movement through her involvement with the Esperance dancers.

Lady Isabel became an active WSPU speaker. She defended letterbox burning, (proclaiming it a lesson to those too stupid to listen to reason), and tax resistance until women had the same influence over government spending as male taxpayers. In 1912, she told *The Standard* that 'we suffragettes' had been forced by the government into militant tactics and that for those like herself who were unable to join in the fight there would be undying regret as well as shame that they had not had the honour of suffering with those brave women who counted liberty worth any sacrifice. In 1914, she chaired a WSPU meeting in Glasgow where Mrs Pankhurst was rearrested amongst turbulent scenes. Her daughter Catherine 'Kitty' Margesson attended Cambridge University (where as a woman she was unable to take a degree), and became the WSPU's organiser in Reading. In January 1910, Kitty ran the WSPU's response to the general election campaign in Redhill in Surrey.

At the end of the First World War, Lady Isabel was one of the founding committee members of the Women's Institute, an organisation into which many former suffrage campaigners later channelled their energies.

Blanche Payling

Born in 1891, Blanche Payling was typical of the Esperance girls. Her father was a packer, her brother a metal polisher and her younger sister, Grace, was an errand girl.

Like Florrie Warren, Payling travelled the country teaching. While staying with Lady Muriel Paget she taught the wife of the Home Secretary. In 1911, Mary sent her to Thaxted in Essex at the invitation of the vicar and his wife. Twenty-year-old Blanche taught three classes a day. When she returned with Mary later in the year, sixty local children demonstrated what she had taught them at the town flower show and an article she had written on the history of the dance revival appeared in the parish magazine. In 1913, Blanche travelled with Mary to Ireland where she taught the assembled company of the annual musicians' study week.

In 1921, Blanche married pub landlord William Henry Dowling. She died in 1935, at the age of 44.

Laurence Housman

Mary said that were it not for Laurence Housman she doubted the national Morris revival would have come about. It is unknown in what capacity Housman first came into contact with Mary and Emmeline, but he moved in similar progressive, activist circles and was invited to the

Esperance Christmas party in 1906 at which the girls first performed for an audience. Housman was enthralled. Prophesising a great revival, he urged Mary to share what she had discovered with the wider world, which led to the performances at the Queen's Hall the following spring.

Housman was a successful writer and illustrator who had contributed to the *Yellow Book*, which brought him into contact with Evelyn Sharp, Cecil Sharp's suffragette sister. His siblings were the poet A.E. Housman and the artist and wood engraver Clemence Housman, a militant suffragette. Like Mary and Emmeline, Housman was a committed campaigner for the vote for women. In June 1908, he designed the banner carried by the Kensington WSPU at the Hyde Park rally. In 1909, he and Clemence were founder members of the Suffrage Atelier. Unlike its counterpart, the Artist's Suffrage League, the Suffrage Atelier was closely allied to the militant movement and members supported the cause by designing banners, posters, postcards and other promotional material. The Housmans' Kensington studio became the Atelier's banner-making headquarters. Several of Housman's suffrage-supporting plays were performed by the Actresses' Franchise League, and he produced a verse book, *The Anti-Suffrage Alphabet*, which was illustrated by Leonora Tyson of the Kensington WSPU and sold to raise funds for the cause.

It was Housman who devised the plan to boycott the 1911 census, which he promoted in print, and made his studio available to women evading the census enumerators. A founder member of the Men's League for Women's Suffrage and the Men's Political Union for Women's Enfranchisement, he was banned from speaking at WSPU meetings in 1913 after joining the National Union of Women's Suffrage Societies' Election Fighting Fund committee which had been formed to support Labour candidates in by-elections. (It was WSPU policy not to support any political party.) That same year, he joined the NUWSS Suffrage Pilgrimage, which brought women on foot and on bicycle to London from across the country. In 1914, he joined Mary, Emmeline and Evelyn Sharp in the newly formed United Suffragists and designed their banner. During the First World War, Housman became a pacifist, writing for Sylvia Pankhurst's *Workers' Dreadnought* magazine.

Chapter Four

'Merrie England once more': Dancing for the Cause 1908–1909

I n the wake of the split in Mrs Pankhurst's WSPU there
was a change in the relationship between the two people
who had done so much to promote the understanding
of the Morris and to popularise it. With the departure of
several high-profile dissenting voices, the Pankhursts and
Pethick-Lawrences were free to pursue their radical strategy
without opposition or challenge. Mary became a member of
the new national organising committee, alongside Emmeline,
Mrs Pankhurst and Christabel, Mabel Tuke and Elizabeth
Robins. The national committee was legally responsible for the
activities of members but seldom met. While Mrs Pankhurst
toured the country, Fred, Emmeline and Christabel decided
day-to-day tactics and long-term strategy. Over the winter
of 1908/9, 3,000 meetings were held across the country.
Hundreds were arrested at set-piece demonstrations when
women refused to be diverted from their objectives and were
charged with obstruction. Arrests and imprisonments brought
the organisation publicity, converts and money. Though
the campaign of civil disobedience would seem to have no
obvious connection to the Morris, it had an impact on the
relationship between Mary Neal and Cecil Sharp. He saw the
promotion of folk song and dance as a means of promoting

social cohesion; the radical suffrage movement had produced social disorder. He was unnerved by the increasing militancy and at the presence of three of those closely involved in the dance revival – Mary, Emmeline and Mabel Tuke – on the WSPU's organising committee, and embarrassed by his own sister's involvement. The appearance of the young dancers at suffrage events, bringing the dances into the political arena, surely dismayed him.

In November 1907, as the WSPU was reforming its structure, Mary convened a meeting at the Goupil Gallery. Chaired by the artist Neville Lytton, the purpose of the meeting was to bring together various interested parties with a view to establishing an organisation to promote the dances nationwide. The day before that meeting, on 13 November, *Punch* magazine published a cartoon captioned 'Merrie England Once More!' It depicted Mr Punch leading a troupe of Morris dancers, male and female through a village. The sub-caption read: 'In consequence of the great success of the Esperance Girls' Club in promoting the revival of English Folksongs and Morris Dances in country villages, a Conference is to be held, on November 14, at the Goupil Gallery for the purpose of furthering this admirable scheme.'

Mary first heard of the cartoon via a telegram from a friend congratulating her on the appearance of the dancers in a national magazine. On purchasing a copy, she was rather thrilled. (The original *Punch* drawing was presented to her at an Esperance concert on 28 November.) But when she showed it to Sharp he was less than pleased. A blind, she said, came over his face and he announced that he would not attend the conference. But what did Sharp object to in the term 'Merrie England'? It was often used as shorthand to depict the England of Shakespeare as a lost rural idyll, a time before low agricultural wages and precarious livings had prompted mass movement to the new cities. A nostalgic vision of Shakespearean England, where ordinary folk lived in spiritual and social harmony was promulgated throughout the late nineteenth and early twentieth centuries by artists and writers as an antidote to the grim realities of urban industrialisation. Dancing was often used in productions of Shakespeare's plays and in historical pageants to suggest the gaiety of this mythical golden age when England was allegedly truly 'merrie'. Mary had no objection to the notion; in fact, she saw herself as making that myth a reality for the most disadvantaged in society, taking young people from the London slums and introducing them to a life of productive work and recreation. The Esperance was demonstrating the fun to be had through song and dance and, in its way, recreating that 'merrie' England. Sharp, however, saw the epithet as encompassing all that he had begun to question about the Esperance. For him, the enjoyment of the dancers was less important than the respect due to the authenticity and integrity of the dances themselves.

Neville Lytton was accompanied to the conference by his sister, Lady Constance Lytton. The siblings were from an influential and well-connected family which demonstrates the social reach of the dance movement. Their late father had been Viceroy of India and their brother sat in the House of Lords. Lady Constance had received an inheritance and after hearing about the Esperance and the Morris revival from her brother she had decided to donate the legacy to the club. It was a decision which she later said marked the beginning of her spiritual life. It also led her to the campaign for the vote – and to prison.

Mary had convened the conference in order to put the case for the formation of a national association dedicated to the promotion of Morris dance. The Esperance Club dancers, she reported, were about to give their eighth concert at Queen's Hall; two girls had retired from their employment entirely and were now travelling the country giving lessons; and another seven or eight were teaching in London. She was getting so many requests that she could not keep up with the demands of the revival. If, as was now proposed, the dances were to be promoted in schools there would be too much administration and management for one small organisation. And if Mary was to head an initiative to spread the dance to communities nationwide she would need to demonstrate her status within the revival. She would be taken more seriously as the head of a dedicated national organisation than as the leader of a London girls' club. She set out her vision of dancing being reintroduced in parks and open spaces, of teachers going out into poor law union and industrial schools, and of city companies funding the revival. The new society would need a paid secretary and funds for promotion and expenses. It would also, Mary told the audience, be in a position to 'guard the purity of the Folk-music'. She feared ignorant people calling all manner of performance 'Morris'; a recognised society would be able to award certificates to teachers that it had trained and who could be relied upon to teach authentic dances. She was not proposing anything academic, she stressed, nothing 'text-book' or dull, but simple, jolly and homely dances for the average boy or girl.

Mary was supported in her proposals by Herbert McIlwaine and Edward Burrows, the inspector of schools from Sussex, who told the assembled audience how dance teaching had taken off there. In her autobiography, Mary recalls Sharp's contribution that evening as 'unhelpful', but Neville Lytton's notes of the meeting record only a curious (and possibly humorous) speech in which Sharp asserted that before Mary came along he had been 'flourishing in the role prophet … prophesying in the Daily Press and the columns of the *Morning Post* as to what Folk Song could do and receiving the pleasure and emoluments attached to that position'. The Esperance, he said, had proved him correct and ruined him as a prophet and forced him to retire from the role! There was an element of pique in his claim that he had taken down some dance tunes seven or eight years previously and tried to get clubs to take them up but nobody had been interested until the Esperance Club set everything alight. But though he was claiming a prior stake in the dance revival, his words gave no indication that a major feud was brewing and he agreed that the new association's purpose should be popularisation of the dance rather than academic study.

The meeting resolved that a society be formed for the development of the practice of English folk music in dance and song. Referring to the 'charming' cartoon in *Punch*, Mary announced that the magazine's proprietor, Laurence Bradbury, had agreed to take the role of treasurer. Mary, Emmeline,

Neville Lytton, Lady Constance, Burrows and McIlwaine were amongst those elected to the provisional committee. But matters did not progress smoothly. At a subsequent meeting, Sharp argued for a detailed constitution so that the proceedings and objects of the new association could be strictly controlled. He was at the time in dispute with the English Folk Song Society whose simple constitution made control of initiatives problematic; he did not want the same flexibility to prevail in the new dance society. Mary, with her commitment to participation and inclusivity, may not have realised what was afoot, but Sharp had experience of enthusiasts forming themselves into a formal organisation. A structure and hierarchy was being created for the dance movement and he foresaw that a new national society with a wide-ranging remit would attempt to formalise standards and determine what was to be regarded as suitable practice and what frivolous or outlandish and therefore to be regarded as outside the 'official' canon. If anyone was to codify what was suitable for teaching and performance nationwide, Sharp wanted it to be him. He argued that the society should be dedicated to promotion, and not to collecting of dances, which should be undertaken by 'experts'. Others argued for the freedom of a simpler and vaguer constitution.

The fledgling committee was unable to come to any agreement. Without a clear constitution the initiative stalled. In frustration, Mary and a few of her associates formed the less ambitious Association for the Revival and Practice of Folk Music with the aim of spreading the dance revival outside the

Esperance Club. Mary pledged not to collect new dances in an attempt to placate Sharp. But, she later recalled:

> From that day, began a bitter attack by Mr. Sharp on the work we were trying to do … Until then there had been no criticism of the dancing, no suggestion of their not being in the tradition and faithfully carrying that tradition. From the hour when the Committee decided to break up as we could come to no decision, the whole atmosphere changed. Mr. Sharp openly challenged everything we did.

Sharp began to express concerns that Mary valued enthusiasm over 'authenticity' and performance over accuracy. This is perhaps not surprising as Morris dancing had never been the traditional preserve of women. She wanted to get people dancing, whilst he was of a more academic disposition. The press tended to support the less rigorous but more inclusive 'Merrie England' approach; in June 1908, the *Musical Times* reported boys dancing with Esperance girls in bright village costumes with bells and stovepipe hats, with great enthusiasm. 'The tiny mites,' the paper reported, 'touched all hearts.'

Sharp also had misgivings at Mary's emphasis on the role of dance in social reform. She saw dance as a means to promote social inclusivity, by giving confidence and a sense of belonging to the socially excluded girls of the urban poor. Sharp was uncomfortable at the use of dance as a tool for social empowerment. He saw the dance as something pure, not as a tool to be used for political purposes and certainly not something that should play any role in changing society. And he was unsettled by the dancers' connection with the campaign for women's political empowerment that was regularly unfolding on the streets of London as women grew more strident in demanding the vote. He expressed his misgivings about Mary and McIlwaine's approach to authenticity to Neville Lytton who brushed off his concerns, advising that if he wanted to popularise the dance he would find plenty of people ready to get involved compared to whom 'McIlwaine is a purist of the deepest dye'. In Lytton's eyes, any liberties Mary and McIlwaine took with interpretations of the dance were minor. Though Sharp had strong opinions on the dance, he was by no means an expert at this stage. He now began collect dances as well as songs, and the more he collected, the more he felt able to set out his standards. In August 1908, he told McIlwaine that the Morris as danced by the Esperance was too flamboyant and 'decorative'. He wanted something 'much more dignified and reticent'. Some of these comments appear to have particular relevance to the female dancers and his opinion on what was and was not appropriate for young women.

With his concerns about dignity and reticence, Sharp could not approve the step up in militant tactics being promoted by the leadership of the suffragette campaign with whom he was collaborating. It is often said that Mary was not an active militant, that she assisted Emmeline in purely domestic and personal ways but had no real commitment to the cause. This is not true. In September 1908, she wrote the first of many long pieces in *Votes for Women*. In November, she donated her speaker's fee from an event in St Andrews to WSPU funds. (Like Emmeline, she was never reluctant to put her own money into her causes.) Perhaps of greater concern as far as Sharp was concerned, was that the Esperance girls danced at suffrage events and both Emmeline and Mary drew on their experience of the dance and the lives of the dancers in their speeches and articles, allying the dance revival in the public mind to the WSPU. In June 1908, Emmeline proudly told a huge crowd from a platform in Hyde Park that she was president of the Esperance Club, whose 'charming' displays of Morris dancing and English folk songs had delighted the nation. In speeches and articles, Mary and Emmeline wove the history of the Esperance Club into that of the women's suffrage movement.

Perhaps Mary's most significant contribution to the campaign for the vote was in those she was able to bring to the cause, several of them directly from the Esperance. Esther Knowles was the daughter of a trades unionist print-worker; her older sister Ellen was an Esperance dancer. Dressed in white with a green sash, 13-year-old Esther walked with the children's contingent to a suffrage rally at the Albert Hall in 1910 and sold *Votes for Women* outside. Her father hit her mother for allowing her to take part. Esther went on to the WSPU payroll and worked in its offices, eventually becoming Fred Pethick-Lawrence's personal secretary. Another young working-class woman who was drawn into the campaign through Mary and Emmeline was May Start. May began life in the London millinery trade and went to work for Fred and Emmeline as a teenager in 1901. In 1906, she was one of the first Esperance dancers, performing in Maidenhead. She taught traditional games to the Esperance children and became Emmeline and Fred's housekeeper, responsible for the practicalities of life in their London and country homes. After 1910, when hunger strikes became a feature of the campaign, May, who was often known as 'Mai Mai', was charged with taking care of recuperating suffragettes in Surrey. The WSPU's secretary, Mabel Tuke, was also now fully involved with the dancers, collecting dances from the Hemmings family in Abingdon for Mary.

By 1908, the struggle to win the vote for women had intensified. Campbell Bannerman had been replaced as prime minister by Henry Herbert Asquith who was implacably opposed though many in his party, as in the Lords and the country in general, were in favour. Huge rallies and marches had attracted thousands of supporters, but there had been no move from government to concede the women's demands. To many it seemed that persuasion had failed and that more radical measures were necessary to persuade government that women would not take no for an answer. There were many supporters, however – both men and women – who were either passive, or who belonged to one or other of the many suffrage organisations which did not advocate militant action. One such was Lady Constance Lytton who was from a suffrage-supporting family but had not involved herself in the campaign. She was now volunteering her services as a pianist for the Esperance and had arranged for the dancers to visit to her family home at Knebworth to teach the villagers there.

In the summer of 1908, 'Lady Connie', who was a great favourite with the girls, was invited to the club's summer holiday at the Green Lady in Littlehampton. She arrived with her brother and the artist Geoffroy Duchaume. There she met Emmeline and the somewhat notorious Annie Kenney who was holidaying with the Esperance. A good number of the Green Lady's guests that summer had been involved in militant activity. But Lady Constance claimed that she had no idea when she volunteered to help that the Esperance Club's founders were suffragettes, perhaps because Emmeline was no longer involved in the day-to-day running of the club, so this was their first real meeting, and Mary's workload with the dance revival precluded regular campaigning. Lady Constance saw Mary and Emmeline as inspirational figures from the outset:

> I realised at once that I was face to face with women of strong personality, and I felt, at first vaguely, that they represented something more than themselves, a force greater than their own seemed behind them. Their remarkable individual powers seemed illumined and enhanced by a light that was apart from them as are the colours and patterns of a stained-glass window by the sun shining through it.

The girls sang on wet days and danced and posed for Duchaume and Neville Lytton. It was only when Annie Kenney's sister, Jessie (who was Emmeline's secretary), came to talk about her time in Holloway prison that Lady Constance realised that she had fallen amongst militant women. By her account she was not pleased at the discovery. But she had a long talk with the highly persuasive Emmeline, whom she described as 'lovable and sympathetic', whilst out on a motoring expedition. On her return to London, she wrote to a friend from the waiting room at Kings Cross station that she had 'got knotted up with suffragettes'. On 14 October, she visited the WSPU's offices to offer her services. On 28 October, Emmeline Pethick-Lawrence wrote a characteristically effusive letter welcoming Lady Constance to the cause.

In November 1908, Lady Constance spoke at a suffrage meeting in Cobham. In December, she walked alongside the notorious Brackenbury sisters to the breakfast celebrations for the release of Mrs Pankhurst and Christabel from prison. Then, at the age of nearly 40 and in somewhat delicate health, Lady Constance determined upon active campaigning. In February 1909, she took part in her first delegation to Parliament. Delegations could be rowdy affairs as women marched in groups towards the House of Commons and tried to speak in the environs whilst being pushed back by the police. Lady Constance lunched beforehand at the WSPU's headquarters with Mary, Emmeline and the Pankhursts and then marched alongside Emmeline. Both were arrested for refusing to be turned back. On refusal to be bound over to keep the peace, they were sentenced to a month in Holloway. Because of her status, however, and with the officers of the law aware of her powerful friends, Lady Constance was released early.

Although Mary was involved in marches in the autumn of 1908, when she accompanied Emmeline and Lady Constance on her first march on Parliament she avoided arrest. She was

Advertisement for the Neal family button-manufacturing business in Birmingham, 1849.

Left to right: Mary Neal, Emmeline Pethick-Lawrence and Lady Constance Lytton outside the Green Lady hostel in Littlehampton where Lady Constance was persuaded to join the militant suffragette movement. Emmeline appears to be wearing a ribbon in the WSPU colours of purple green and white. (The Women's Library, London School of Economics)

Emmeline Pethick-Lawrence. (WSPU postcard, the People's History Museum NMLH 2001.1.15)

Right: Mary Neal in 1910. (Institute of Archaeology, Oxford University)

Below: Mary Neal in later life. (Lucy Neal)

Left: Emmeline Pethick-Lawrence (driving), May Start (far left) and children of the Esperance Club holidaying at the Pethick-Lawrences' home in Surrey. (Dorking Museum)

Below: Small girls of the Esperance Children's Club dancing on Holmwood Common near the Pethick-Lawrences' Surrey home. (Museum of London)

Above: The Sundial, the holiday home that the Pethick-Lawrences built for the Esperance Club in Holmwood, Surrey. (Dorking Museum)

Right: Lady Constance Lytton. (WSPU postcard from the collection of Ann Lewis and Mike Sponder)

May Start, the Pethick-Lawrences' housekeeper outside The Sundial in Holmwood. May danced with the Esperance and taught singing games to the Esperance children. (*The Esperance Morris Book part 1*)

Laurence Housman, the male suffrage supporter who first suggested to Mary that the Esperance perform for the public. (Library of Congress)

Florence 'Florrie' Warren. (*The Esperance Morris Book part 1*)

Suffragette leaders Mabel Tuke (left) and Emmeline Pethick-Lawrence. (Women's Library, London School of Economics)

Emmeline Pethick-Lawrence (left) and Mabel Tuke (centre) with Israel Zangwill leading a WSPU procession. (Women's Library, London School of Economics)

Emmeline Pankhurst and Emmeline Pethick-Lawrence lead the Women's Coronation Procession on 17 June 1911, followed by Christabel Pankhurst and Mabel Tuke. (The Women's Library, London School of Economics)

Emmeline Pethick-Lawrence (centre) marching in the Prison to Citizenship Procession on June 18 1910 alongside Christabel Pankhurst (left) and Mrs Pankhurst (right). Lady Constance Lytton can be seen behind Emmeline's shoulder and Mabel Tuke at the front. (The Women's Library, London School of Economics)

Left to right: Mabel Tuke, Mrs Pankhurst and Emmeline and Frederick Pethick-Lawrence in the dock at the preliminary hearing of their trial for conspiracy, 14 March 1912. (The Women's Library, London School of Economics)

The National Women's
Social & Political Union.

OFFICE:

4, CLEMENTS INN, STRAND, W.C.

Telegraphic Address—"WOSPOLU, LONDON."   Telephone 5550 Holborn

Committee:

Mrs. PANKHURST,   Mrs. PETHICK LAWRENCE,
Founder and Hon. Sec.   *Hon. Treasurer.*
Mrs. TUKE,   Miss CHRISTABEL PANKHURST,
Joint Hon. Sec.   *Organising Sec.*

Mrs. WOLSTENHOLME ELMY.   Miss MARY E. GAWTHORPE.
Miss ANNIE KENNEY.   Mrs. N. A. MARTEL.
Miss MARY NEAL.   Miss ELIZABETH ROBINS.

Auditor: A. G. SAYERS, Chartered Accountant, 19, Hanover Square, W.
Bankers: Messrs. BARCLAY & Co., 19, Fleet Street, E.C.

Above left: Evelyn Sharp. (Wikimedia Commons)

Above right: WSPU official header, post 1907.

PUNCH, OR THE LONDON CHARIVARI.—November 13, 1907.

MERRIE ENGLAND ONCE MORE!

[In consequence of the great success of the Espérance Girls' Club in promoting the revival of English Folksongs and Morris Dances in country villages, a Conference is to be held, on November 14, at the Goupil Gallery for the purpose of furthering this admirable scheme. (See article on page 347.)]

The 'Merrie England' Punch cartoon published on 13 November 1907 that marked the beginning of the rift between Cecil Sharp and Mary Neal. (Author's own collection)

THE FIRST TWO WHO SET OUT TO TEACH.

Above left: Cecil Sharp, the folk song expert who clashed with Mary about her methods and interpretation of the Morris dance. (Library of Congress)

Above right: The first two Esperance teachers, Florrie Warren and Blanche Payling from a piece written by Mabel Tuke for *Votes for Women*, 15 September 1911. (*Votes for Women*, Royal Holloway archive)

Below: Esperance girls demonstrating the Morris at the Stratford Festival. (The Shakespeare Revival)

THE DAILY MIRROR.

TEACHING THE MORRIS DANCE ON A HOUSE ROOF.

London workgirls are now teaching the Morris dance in their spare moments, and make as much as 12s. 6d. a week in addition to their ordinary wages. The photographs show a dancing lesson being given on the roof of a flat near St. Pancras Church.

Left: The Esperance girls teaching on the roof of Mary's flat in St Pancras. (*The Daily Mirror*)

Below: William Trafford teaches the Esperance girls on his visit to London in November 1910. (*The Daily Mirror*)

FAMOUS MORRIS DANCER TEACHES LONDONERS TO BE MERRY.

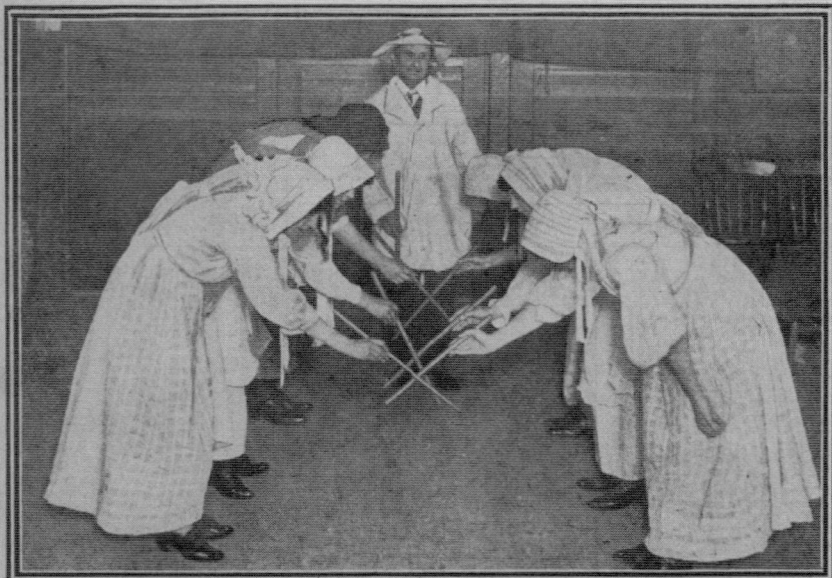

Mr. William Trafford, aged seventy-four, a celebrated dancer, of Hedington Quarry, Oxfordshire, who came to Crosby Hall, Chelsea, to teach the Esperance Guild of Morris Dancers. Above, he is seen giving some pupils a lesson. He had never been in London before, and got lost on the "Underground."—(*Daily Mirror* photograph.)

Three photos of the Esperance dancers. (*The Esperance Morris Book part 2*)

Another picture of the dancers and their fiddler. The "fool" (in the middle of the back line), following tradition, is supposed to be the best dancer. Originally, of course, Morris-Dances were danced by men alone

Esperance dancers in Elizabethan costume for the Earls Court Exhibition in the summer of 1912. (*The Bystander*)

An ESSAY in PATRIOTISM : TEACHING FOLK-MUSIC TO CHILDREN

A MORRIS DANCER practising with a broom-handle.

"GRACE IN EVERY GESTURE AND A SMILE ON EVERY FACE". A STUDY OF DIMINUTIVE FEMININITY
All the pictures on this page, except this one, are reproduced by permission of the Espérance Club.

AN APT PUPIL, who has taught many of the children.

Above and below: Children of the Esperance Club and older dancers featured in Mary's article in *The Graphic* 5 February 1910. (*The Graphic*)

"SHEPHERDS' AYE," or "Shepherds' Hey," danced by the older members of the Espérance Club.

"BEAN-SETTING," a very old, traditional tune and dance. The knees of the dancers—here shown in costume—are covered with small metal bells.

"MORRIS ON." The dancers enter to this tune, using the characteristic gesture here shown.

Emmeline Pethick-Lawrence with kinsmen of the Kibbo Kift in home-made Saxon hoods at Lincoln's Inn in 1922. (London School of Economics Library)

Above: Mary Neal with her friend Richard Lowe Thompson at an archaeological excavation at Botley Copse in 1910. He described her as 'everything a good aunt should be'. (Institute of Archaeology, Oxford University)

Left: The feet of Esperance dancers by Sylvia Pankhurst. She made a series of studies of the girls' feet for a painting of the dancers in action. Sylvia was a close friend of Emmeline Pethick-Lawrence; the two were imprisoned together in 1906. (Helen Pankhurst)

balancing her campaigning activities with the demands of the dancers. But she remained an active campaigner; in September she travelled to Newcastle where she chaired a WSPU meeting with Mrs Pankhurst. The meeting was lively; men were thrown downstairs in scuffles beforehand. But Mary's experience, from her Mission days, of dealing with trouble made her adept at dealing with such threats. Fearing the stage would be stormed, she stood behind her leader, offering the petite Mrs Pankhurst physical protection while she spoke. She later recalled her fear that had she taken her eye off the crowd for a second, they would have stampeded. After the event, high-profile prisoners recently released from Holloway – amongst them Nellie Martel, Elsie Howey, Vera Wentworth and Florence Haig – were paraded through the city streets.

On 17 September, another of Mary's pieces appeared in *Votes for Women*. In 'Here's a prisoner we have got' she wove an account of an Esperance holiday into her vision of the militant suffrage movement. The piece was probably based on the recent summer holiday at the Green Lady at which Lady Constance had been converted to the cause. Mary describes the Sussex Downs ablaze with poppies, yellow corn and cornflowers, and an old-fashioned garden with medlar and walnut trees, amongst which was 'a company of merry London children, playing old English singing games'. They play them, she says, for 'all the sparkle and mischief in their eyes', but as if they still have some spiritual connection with the past through the songs. The description is spiritual, but her conclusions are practical. She explains that when the children play 'London Bridge is Falling Down' they recite lines about a man who is imprisoned when he is unable to pay the fine for stealing a watch. This game, she says, is based on an old belief that no bridge will stand unless its foundations are built on human sacrifice. She goes on to make a direct connection between the blood sacrifice required to make a bridge stand and the scenes in London, where processions of women prepare to sacrifice themselves:

> They know the life of the nation is incomplete, that the bridge between the law-makers and those who live under the laws is broken and are going to ask to help rebuilding that bridge. They know all the usual ways – strength, gold etc. are futile, but the only thing that will be effective is the gift of human life.

She draws a somewhat forced analogy between the children's folk game and the radical movement for political reform. There is no achievement without sacrifice, she tells her readers, no building will stand the stress of time without human life at its foundation. Her vision of the future is a bridge built on the sacrifice of women, a bridge of laws made by all and therefore obeyed by all. In such pieces, Mary is directly promoting the WSPU's veneration of sacrifice to her readers and drawing on her knowledge of folk dance and traditional games to encourage the bodily sacrifice of women for the cause. In the months and years to come women would take inspiration from her words and from similar pieces by Emmeline and the Pankhursts. Very soon prisons would see women not just incarcerated, but refusing food and being forcibly fed. Some would die for the cause.

In October, Mary was back with the dancers, speaking at a festival in Oxford and offering classes to teachers on how to teach. If the dances continued to be so popular, she told her audience, it would indeed become Merrie England! But the rift with Sharp was deepening as Mary became more involved with the WSPU. In November he wrote to fellow folk song collector Lucy Broadwood – whose sister Bertha led her local branch of the Women's League for Opposing Women's Suffrage – disassociating himself from the Esperance. He 'deprecated very strongly', he told Lucy, the impertinent assumption of the Esperance that they originated the whole folk dance movement. He also expressed his concerns that Mary wished to take control of the revival to William Kimber, the Oxfordshire bricklayer who had taught the first dances to the Esperance. 'She isn't satisfied with having a ride in the conveyance,' Kimber reported him saying, 'she wants the reins.' Sharp was concerned that his position as 'the' folk expert was in jeopardy. Mary was inviting dancers from the provinces to London to teach her girls, not men like Kimber who were known to Sharp, but others whose traditions he did not know and who he could not influence. He saw Mary as coming late to the folk revival that he had initiated; but where the dance was concerned, she saw herself as being the one who had taken the initiative first and as being as much in the driving seat as Sharp.

In January 1909, Sharp expressed concerns to Neville Lytton about an article entitled 'Dancing and Social Reform: What London working girls are doing' which Mary had written for the *Morning Post*. In it she inextricably linked the story of the dance revival with that of the Esperance in her typically mystical and romantic manner. Seeing this, Sharp quite possibly felt himself in danger of being written out of the history of the dance revival. On 7 March, he wrote to Mary, accusing her of taking stories that he had told about folk song and singers and claiming them for her own glory and that of the Esperance. He also accused her of posing as an authority, which must have perplexed Mary since she could very reasonably claim expertise in the dance. And he suggested that her dancers' performances were not true to the original dances. His greatest desire, he told her, was that 'at the outset these songs and dances should be introduced to the present generation in the purest form possible'. Mary's girls, he suggested, were embellishing or degrading the dances. Mary tried to placate him and to maintain their working relationship but Sharp made it clear that he would no longer support her.

Given his antipathy to the suffrage movement, the activities of the dancers during this period could only have unsettled him further. In March 1909, Emmeline explained to readers of *Votes for Women* that she had been on direct road to prison from the formation of the Esperance Club. It was the tide of human misery that had swept past her door when she worked with Mary, she claimed, that had driven her to militant action. She was once more in Holloway, having been arrested in February after a breach of the peace on a deputation to the House of Commons. From her prison cell, she issued directions on arrangements for a demonstration at the Albert Hall planned for April, urging members to sell tickets and to raise the £50,000 that she had set as a fundraising target for the year.

Her tone in the one letter per month that she was permitted to write was uplifting, celebrating her 'wonderful movement'. 'Nothing seems too much to hope, too great to believe and expect,' she told her followers, with spring bringing life and joy back into the world. 'We will give body and soul and all that we have to minister to this new life,' she wrote, of the shoots of the suffrage campaign. 'We will accomplish the purpose to which we have been called ... in the strong bond of fellowship which unites us all in the movement.' While Emmeline was in prison Mrs Pankhurst appealed to readers of *Votes for Women* for contributions to buy a car in WSPU colours for the use of 'our devoted treasurer'. The prisoner emerged from Holloway on 16 April to a rapturous reception of 1,000 people, a car in suffragette colours and a celebratory breakfast for 400 at the Criterion restaurant. The next day she was led in a procession headed by a supporter dressed as Joan of Arc from Hyde Park to the Aldwych. The Esperance girls accompanied her, marching alongside her prison companions, part of a long procession of women marching in step four-abreast, followed by bands and holding banners.

Cecil Sharp and Mary Neal sat with McIlwaine on the judging panel for the folk dancing competitions at the Stratford folk festival in early May 1909. Though they interacted politely in public, Sharp distanced himself from the Esperance, avoiding their performances. On 6 May, Mary wrote to him from her hotel room, attempting a reconciliation. She reminded him of the early years of their friendship and how much they had in common, regretting the 'misunderstandings' that had come between them and urging him to come and talk to her. She was leaving the festival full of ideas. 'The work must go on,' she told him, 'and it is a thousand pities not to do it together.'

A few days later, the Esperance girls turned out in support of the suffrage cause once again, dancing at the WSPU's Women's Exhibition held at the Prince's Skating Rink in Knightsbridge. The exhibition was a two-week-long celebration of women's abilities and achievements in all areas of life. The appearances of the Esperance dancers contributed to the exhibition's joyful and celebratory atmosphere. But Sharp was now not the only one uncomfortable with the dancers' visible involvement in the militant movement. Mary's close collaborator, Herbert McIlwaine, resigned as the Esperance Club's musical director, ostensibly on account of ill-health. Privately, Mary knew that he did not want to be associated with the suffragette leadership. His departure must have been a considerable blow to her. Lady Constance took over McIlwaine's role until the appointment of Clive Carey as the club's musical director. A singer as well as a folk song collector, Carey often sang at Esperance events and accompanied Mary out into the countryside in search of new material. (He went on to become an opera producer and director and taught at the Royal College of Music.)

In June, the Esperance dancers appeared in Oxford with William Kimber. The *Oxford Chronicle and Reading Gazette* reported that they 'seemed to convey something of the lost joy of the countryside which was burned out in the fierce fire of industrialism; they were so essentially English from beginning to end'. The piece illustrates a theme which Mary did not discourage. The dance revival was not just about reviving a lost heritage but that heritage was asserted to be 'essentially'

English, as if the idyllic and the rural were unquestionably English but the horrors of modern capitalism as manifested in London's slums were not equally so. For Mary, whose words surely fed into the piece, the soul of 'Englishness' meant equality and quality of life. Somehow those English values had been abandoned and must be reclaimed. In words that would not have amused Cecil Sharp, and which might have been from Mary's pen, the piece concluded that the dances summed up the spirit of 'Merrie England' 'when men made things for use and not for sale and delighted in the countryside rather than the glamour of the large towns'.

In July, the Esperance were in Solihull in the West Midlands performing to raise money to fund a Midlands-based organiser for the (non-militant) NUWSS. Florrie Warren had travelled up in advance to teach local children. According to the local paper, the girls' performances caused 'even the Anti-suffragists present to go away feeling glad that they had given their money in aid of the Society'! On 9 August, another long piece by Mary appeared in *Votes for Women*. In 'The Wisdom of the Folk' Mary retells a harvest folk tale of the lone sheaf containing the spirit of the wheat that must be buried in the earth to ensure the next harvest. Through the suffering of this 'John Barleycorn', a Christlike figure who is ploughed into the earth only to rise up again, year after year, wheat is the life-giving food of man. This, Mary claims, is a truth known to country folk but not to 'bookmen'. Is this perhaps a dig at Sharp, with his book knowledge of the dance, but lack of appreciation of the spirit of the dance? As in her piece the previous autumn, Mary draws a direct analogy between death in the folk tradition and the way that the women of 1909 were sacrificing themselves in the fight for liberty of body, soul and spirit. Women, she suggests, are unconsciously emulating John Barleycorn, and women, she asserts, are nearer to the Earth Mother than men: 'wiser in the wisdom learned at the gates of death as each life is born at the gates of death'. Women have 'committed the seeds of liberty to the earth; ploughed in by suffering, it has been ruthlessly cut down again and again, condemned to death by the Kings of Prejudice, Tyranny and Lust, and risen triumphant'. But now, she claims, in the suffragette movement, 'the harvest is near at hand'. Mary takes a masculine character from national folk tradition and recasts it to present a feminist message to her readers. And the message is that progress requires sacrifice. Her words were very appealing to an audience of women already giving themselves to prison, and who the following year would embrace the hunger strike.

Cecil Sharp could not forgive Mary for involving the Esperance dancers at suffrage events. He was appalled by the militancy of the women in promotion of their cause and barely kept in touch with his sister Evelyn during her prison experiences. For him, the Esperance dancers were tainted by association with the militants and he began to look for less radical collaborators. But he had other motives for wishing to sideline Mary. Unlike follow collectors such as Ralph Vaughan Williams or Lucy Broadwood, he was not independently wealthy. He could only devote his time to collecting folk songs and dances full time if he could make a living from it. And to do that he needed to establish his credentials as an expert, or 'the' expert in the area. Mary was a threat to him with the

Esperance the nearest thing the movement had to a national body. His efforts to undermine her and the Esperance were to an extent driven by financial necessity as well as his ambition to be recognised as a folklorist. His were very different ambitions from Mary's driving desire to obtain the vote and to create a more equal society for women and the underprivileged.

In the summer of 1909, Sharp made his repudiation of Mary Neal and all she stood for increasingly public. He set out his views in the introduction to the *Esperance Morris Book part 2*, published that August. He also rewrote the introduction to the original 'Morris Book', removing all reference to Mary Neal, Florrie Warren and the Esperance's contribution to the revival. Whereas the original introduction to the first book had stated that the Morris was more about vigour than grace, Sharp now contended that that statement had been too literally interpreted. Dancers now were 'over-strenuous', adopting a 'hoydenish manner of execution', both of which comments could be interpreted as having as much to do with a conservative man seeking to determine what is seemly physical activity for young women as with what might be considered historically 'authentic'. Mary was deeply angered at criticisms of her dancers and told Sharp so. 'I have done with the farce of expecting fair play,' she told him. 'In the future I shall consider myself absolved from all obligations to further the interests of anything or anybody but those of the movement at large and my club in particular.' To which Sharp responded:

That has been the trouble from the beginning of the chapter. You have striven from the first to identify the

movement with your club and to limit your staff of
teachers to the members of your club, to present to
the public no higher artistic standard of performance
than that of which you and your club were capable.
In the administration of your society you deliberately
isolated yourself from and refused to associate
yourself with those who were better acquainted with
the subject than yourself and animated by higher
artistic ideals than your own.

Not only does he accuse her of personal ambition (which in
early twentieth-century society was considered undesirable in
a woman) but he also judges her and her dancers incapable of
'higher artistic ideals'. For a woman who had dedicated her life
to giving girls from the slums access to culture that had been
denied them and who claimed an equality of worth for their lives
and talents, to have her artistic ideals dismissed as inadequate
went against everything she believed. Having accused her of
ambition and dismissed the paucity of her 'artistic ideals',
Sharp was now setting up a rival organisation and he justified
this move on the grounds that Mary's girls were betraying the
dignity of the dance. 'Already the opinion is getting about that
the Morris dance is a graceless, undignified and uncouth dance
quite unfitted for educational uses,' he told her.

It is telling that Sharp was concerned about the place of
the dance in the education system. The opportunity to take
the dance into every community in the country had presented
itself when the Board of Education announced the intention
of publishing a syllabus for physical exercise in schools. If folk

dance were to be adopted in curricula nationwide there would be a huge demand for trained teachers. This offered a career opportunity for Sharp to train those teachers, and the prospect of a regular income. The rivalry between Mary Neal and Cecil Sharp intensified and the debate now became focused on setting official standards and the question of who had the authority and expertise to do so. As soon as the Board of Education published its syllabus for public elementary schools and approved the inclusion of dance in August 1909, Mary wrote to the Board and the *Westminster Gazette* and *Morning Post* pointing out that her teachers were already out travelling the country. She was quick to point out that the Esperance had invited the original traditional dancers back to visit in order to ensure that that 'form and spirit' of the dances as taught by the Esperance remained true to tradition. Sharp, meanwhile, was talking to Edward Burrows about preparing his own teachers and Burrows had arranged a meeting for him with Edmond Holmes, the chief inspector for elementary schools.

To be adopted in schools the dance certainly could not have any whiff of 'hoydenish' impropriety. 'I am not going to stand idly by any longer and allow you to make or mar the fortunes of the movement,' Sharp told Mary. He was now recruiting his own teachers, who, he said, 'in my opinion are far better qualified to spread the Morris than the members of your club.' He did not blame Florrie Warren or her fellow dancers for the situation, he told her, but rather Mary 'for refusing to allow them to be properly directed and controlled'. Mary was appalled by Sharp's dismissal of Florrie. Neville Lytton still hoped for a reconciliation, telling Sharp in September that it would serve the cause better if they worked together, and reiterating in December that it would be a pity not to use Mary's 'propagandist powers'. But the two never worked together again.

Mary's campaigning for the vote stepped up in the late summer and autumn of 1909; on 15 October, Emmeline published another of Mary's articles entitled 'Red Campion' in *Votes for Women*. This time, Mary drew on personal experience to justify the campaign, recalling taking a party of London children to a cottage in the countryside in summer where she filled the room with red campion flowers so that the children would take the memory of its vividness back to their colourless streets as if it were a secret known only to them. In this article she lays out her rage at the conditions of the girls' lives, the toll taken on their youths by long hours in workshops working to support ailing parents and younger siblings. She asserts the value of the individual: 'the stuff that is in them, the peasant ancestry not far from any Londoner, the capacity for health and life-giving happiness, the gift for hard work and unselfish service'. And she sets out her vision for 'a future when these inward qualities could be used for the uplifting of that dreary weight of monochrome drudgery'. From such drudgery the Esperance has provided liberation: 'It is the general awakening which comes as a result of our work which delights me most, the happiness of the children and young folks everywhere.' She does not make the connection between the dance and the campaign for the vote overt but urges her suffrage-supporting readership to attend the demonstration of dancing planned for Kensington Town Hall on 21 October.

The following month, Mary was out once more, speaking at an event run by the Kensington branch of the WSPU at the home of the notoriously militant Brackenbury sisters with Clemence Housman. Lady Constance endeavoured to get herself arrested again in October 1909. She threw a stone wrapped in a slogan at Lloyd George's car in Newcastle and was again given preferential treatment. Prison doctors had been alerted to her heart condition; she was given a medical examination and released without being forcibly fed when she went on hunger strike. High-profile campaigners like Emmeline and Lady Constance received much publicity but newspaper reports did not reflect the suffering, both mental and physical, inflicted upon the majority of those arrested who were of lower social status. Lady Constance was now determined to demonstrate the inequality in treatment of women within the penal system. In January 1910, she dressed herself as a working-class girl to attend a demonstration outside Walton prison in Liverpool, giving the name Jane Wharton on her arrest. This time none of the niceties were observed; there was no medical examination and she was forcibly fed, an excruciating and humiliating process, eight times before her identity was discovered. Her accounts of the brutal treatment of ordinary women in the cells, published in *The Times* and *Votes for Women*, shocked the nation and exposed the government to furious correspondence in the papers.

On leaving prison, Lady Constance was employed as a full-time organiser by WSPU at £2 a week, backdated in acknowledgment of her service in Walton prison. For the first time in her life she had independently earned money. From the stately home of Knebworth, she moved into a rented flat at 15 Somerset Terrace in the heart of St Pancras, the working-class district in which Mary and Emmeline had chosen to set up their club. She became Mary's close neighbour. The new role would mean weekdays away from home but every Friday to Monday was free. 'Wondrous terms. In return I give all I have to give, night and day, year in year out,' she told her Aunt Theresa. The Esperance dancers had been responsible for the revival of a dying dance form, and for bringing the lives of underprivileged girls into the limelight; it is apt that the girls' performances should have inspired the political commitment of a woman who was able to highlight the inequality of treatment endured by working-class women, even when in prison fighting for the most basic of equalities.

Evelyn Sharp (1869–1955)

The actress Elizabeth Robins said that Evelyn Sharp had made 'the biggest sacrifice of time, ambition, health and most of the outward things that sensitive, proud, spirited women prize' in the cause of the vote for women.

Evelyn was Cecil Sharp's youngest sister. Her parents discouraged her from attending university or following a career, but, determined to make a living as a writer, she left the family home and supported herself tutoring until she was able to earn enough from writing to live on. She wrote short stories, children's books and novels and was a contributor to the *Yellow Book*. By 1903, she was writing full time; journalism for papers such as the *Manchester Guardian* paid the bills and enabled her to write fiction. She moved in artistic circles and was friends with fellow dance and suffrage supporter Laurence Housman. She joined the WSPU in 1906 after hearing the actress and WSPU London committee member Elizabeth Robins speak.

Evelyn joined the Kensington WSPU and her sister Bertha took the role of branch secretary. She initially gave a promise to her mother not to take part in any action which might risk imprisonment. Instead, she supported the cause by writing, speaking and organising events and processions. She wrote regularly for *Votes for Women*, prompting Emmeline to write on one occasion congratulating her on a 'quite delicious' article; she later became one of Emmeline's closest friends in the campaign. In 1909, the WSPU sent Evelyn to Denmark to lecture on the militant movement and in 1910 she published *Rebel Women*, a series of stories based on suffragette life.

Evelyn's mother eventually released her from her promise not to undertake any action that might lead to imprisonment. '*Although I hope you will never go to prison,*' wrote Mrs Sharp, '*I feel I ... must really leave it to your better judgement ... I have really been very unhappy about it and feel I have no right to thwart you, much as I should regret feeling that you undergoing those terrible hardships. It has caused you as much pain as it has me, and I feel I can no longer think of my own feeling.*' Evelyn was first arrested in November 1911 and sentenced to fourteen days in Holloway for breaking windows at the War Office. She took over as editor of *Votes for Women* in 1912 when the Pethick-Lawrences were in prison. When Mrs Pankhurst ejected the Pethick-Lawrences from the WSPU in late 1912, Evelyn was torn. For a while she balanced allegiance to the Pethick-Lawrences and the Pankhursts, continuing to jointly edit *Votes for Women* (which the Pethick-Lawrences now ran as an independent suffrage magazine), though she was still a member of the Kensington WSPU. She was also a member of the Women Writer's Suffrage League and in July 1913 she accompanied Emmeline Pethick-Lawrence, as the League's delegate to protest at the use of the Prisoners (Temporary Discharge for Ill-health) Act (more commonly known as the Cat and Mouse Act). She and Emmeline were arrested in the lobby of the House of Commons and she was sentenced to fourteen days, though released early after going on hunger strike.

When the United Suffragists was formed in February 1914, Sharp was a founder member. She took over as sole editor of *Votes for Women* when the Pethick-Lawrences handed the paper to the new organisation.

During the First World War, Evelyn Sharp refused to pay her taxes on the grounds that as a non-voter with no say in the election of those who made the decision to wage war, she ought not have to pay for it. Her household goods were seized by bailiffs on behalf of the tax authorities, though her friends in the suffrage movement, including Mary and Emmeline, clubbed together to replace her home furnishings. She attempted to join Emmeline at the Women's International Peace Conference in neutral Holland in 1915 but was not permitted to travel. In 1917, she was thrilled at the news of the October Revolution in Russia, seeing it as the end of a great tyranny, but she never joined the British Communist Party as she was opposed to the use of force in all circumstances.

After the war, she campaigned with Emmeline to raise the naval blockade on Germany that had led to mass hunger. She worked with the Society of Friends in famine relief in Germany and in post-revolutionary Russia, travelling across the newly formed Soviet Union in terrible winter conditions. She and Emmeline went to Ireland in 1919 at the behest of the Labour Party, at some danger to themselves, to investigate alleged atrocities by the Black and Tans. She also travelled to Germany to report on the rise of Nazism and while she was there she acquainted herself with traditional German folk dancing.

The love of Evelyn Sharp's life was the charismatic war correspondent Henry Nevinson, an active supporter of the vote for women and founder member of the United Suffragists. He regarded her as one of the WSPU's best orators; 'she deployed,' he wrote, 'every sort of wit and eloquence and surprise and insight.' Though their relationship began in 1901, she and Nevinson were unable to marry as he was already (unhappily) married. That she was, therefore, unable to have children was a source of disappointment as she had written many children's books and stories. She and Nevinson's interests in the Labour party, social justice, young people and the dance movement, brought them very close to Emmeline and Fred Pethick-Lawrence and to Mary Neal. Evelyn, Nevinson, Mary and Emmeline were founder members of the Kindred of the Kibbo Kift youth movement in the 1920s.

She and Nevinson were early members of the English Folk Dance Society and sat on its committee in the 1930s. She danced under her brother's direction, on one occasion taking part at the Basque Festival in Bayonne. She was involved in the establishment of Cecil Sharp House as the Society's headquarters, named in memory of her brother, and wrote a history of folk dance. Evelyn Sharp remained close to Mary and Emmeline throughout her life and proofread Fred Pethick-Lawrence's autobiography. She was finally able to marry Nevinson on the death of his wife in 1933, when she was 66 and he was 75.

Esther Knowles

Esther Knowles was one of the St Pancras girls who were drawn into a political life through their association with Mary Neal and the Pethick-Lawrences. She was the daughter of a trades unionist print-worker and as a small child she was a member of the Esperance's club for younger children, holidaying in Holmwood with the newly married Pethick-Lawrences. She and her sisters all danced with the Esperance. Her older sister, Ellen, married one of the young men brought in to dance with the Esperance girls at demonstrations. (Vic Ghirardi became one of Mary's dance teachers and she was godmother to the couple's daughter, Nita.)

Esther's intelligence was recognised by the Pethick-Lawrences and when her father would not allow her to stay on at school, they took the teenager to work in the WSPU offices. During one raid, she stowed the contents of the cashbox in her underwear. She recalled that, 'it was great fun to us young folk though not to our elders. We enjoyed the flitting from one secret hideout to another at the period as the police each time discovered our new whereabouts and we went on to the next secret temporary resting place.'

Esther became Fred's secretary, referring to him as 'Pethick'. She was a trusted member of the Pethick-Lawrences' 'family', working for him throughout his time as an MP and Secretary of State for India, until his death in 1961. She organised the couple's lives in London and Surrey and took her holidays with Emmeline's sister Dorothy, who initiated her into the Steiner philosophy. When she was bombed out of her flat during the Blitz she was resupplied with furniture by Mary, Fred and Emmeline.

It would be hard to overestimate the extent of Esther's lifelong devotion to her employers. She described Emmeline as her 'lodestar'. Fred referred to her as 'an ever-loving friend' and Esther told him that her working life with him had been happy, free and frank, full and complete, and that she had been fortunate as a young girl when destiny had decreed that the path of her life should run alongside his. She was protective of Fred and Emmeline's reputations, during their lives and afterwards, organising a memorial fund and commemorative ceremonies and salvaging many of Emmeline and Mary's papers for posterity.

Esther Knowles died in a car crash in 1974.

Lady Constance Lytton (1869–1923)

Lady Constance Lytton was the daughter of Robert Bulwer Lytton, 1st Earl of Lytton and ex-viceroy of India. Her mother, Edith, her sister Lady Elizabeth 'Betty' Balfour and her brother Victor, the 2nd Earl, were all active non-militant suffrage campaigners, as was her maternal aunt, Maria Theresa Villiers. Her sister-in-law, Lady Frances Balfour, was president of the London Society for Women's Suffrage and sat on the executive committee of the NUWSS. Another sister, Lady Emily Lutyens was an early supporter of the WSPU. Lady Emily left the WSPU after a short time, but later worked with Emmeline as a member of the United Suffragists.

Lady Constance was drawn into the militant campaign for the vote through her activities with the Esperance Club and her support for the Morris revival. She was converted to the cause when holidaying with the dancers at the club's Green Lady hostel in Littlehampton and went on to be an active campaigner, arrested and imprisoned on several occasions. Her ruse of dressing up and claiming to be Jane Wharton, a working-class woman, enabled her to expose the double standards in treatment of women according to their class within the penal system.

Like many who endured the torture of force feeding, Lady Constance never really recovered her health. After suffering a heart attack and a series of strokes that left her paralysed – blamed by her family on the effects of forcible feeding – her activities were severely curtailed. In March 1914, May Start, the Pethick-Lawrences' housekeeper, who had danced and taught games to the young Esperance girls a decade earlier, was instructed by Emmeline to care for Lady Constance while she convalesced at their Surrey home. May, Emmeline assured Lady Constance, would do 'everything to show how you how much we love you'. Lady Constance later recalled that she and her nurse had been 'showered with kindness'.

Lady Constance remained an invalid until her early death in 1923.

Chapter Five

A Bitter Feud: Mary Neal and Cecil Sharp 1910–1911

Mary had a head start over Sharp in the battle for control of the Morris revival. She was a skilled organiser and networker and by 1910 her experienced girls had taught in all but two English counties. Sharp's interest had been more academic and initially confined to song. His status as a music teacher was an advantage as he could claim to be a professional scholar, whereas Mary's background was in social activism; however, he had no organisation to support him. Nor, now he had rejected Mary's methods, was he now able to call on the Esperance dancers to demonstrate figures and footwork at his lectures. So, he established his own School of Morris Dancing at Chelsea College of Physical Education. His aim, he announced, was to conserve the Morris 'in all its traditional purity'. An advertising insert for the new school was placed in every copy of the Morris book. This was necessary, Sharp told the publisher, as though he had been very patient with Mary and tried to keep her on 'proper lines', she was 'quite incurably inaccurate' and apt to deluge the papers with half-true statements about her club and its role in the revival and claims of authority for herself to which, he said, she had no rightful claim at all. He was building up a team to rival the Esperance. When Mary introduced an all-male team, he set out to find one too. But his approach was subtly different to Mary's. The difference was not just in style, but in philosophy.

In February 1910, Mary published 'An Essay on Patriotism' in *The Graphic* magazine. In it, she set out what she believed to be the place of folk dance in national culture. Folk songs and dances, she told her readers, had 'evolved' rather than being composed. This was a direct challenge to Sharp and to the notion that there was a 'correct', immutable form of the dance that could be contained and constrained. Dance had, she wrote, evolved in performance by working people who were in direct contact with the soil. Much of the article is fanciful, asserting that the dance was a 'first-hand musical expression of race' (by which she meant culture and land, rather than skin colour) so that children and townspeople fell under its sway with some sort of 'ancestral memory', unconsciously learning folk songs and dances with ease. But the conclusions she draws are practical: 'Teachers of folk music are now being sent out to every part of the country, and their efforts are sure to bear a large part in quickening the patriotic sense which the pessimists tell us is dead or dying in England.' For Mary the dance is patriotic, but she defines patriotism not as triumphalism, exceptionalism or nationalism but as pride in tradition and heritage. Hers is not a patriotism harnessed for political or military purposes, but a dream of uniting a people with its culture as a means of empowerment and liberation.

In March 1910, Mary formed the Esperance Guild of Morris Dancers, emphasising its much wider remit than promoting the dance in the hope that 'all men and women of good will who wish to see a fair and happier life for the people of England shall belong'. In the same month she published the first *Esperance Morris Book*, which enabled her to claim expertise and authority. Sharp responded by writing to the *Morning Post* on 1 April 1910 to say that he hoped that the promoters – by which he meant Mary and her followers – would allow their enthusiasm to be guided by those who 'possess the requisite experience and knowledge' – by which he meant himself. Mary replied via a letter in *Vanity Fair* on 14 April: 'It behoves those of us to whom has been entrusted the guidance and helping of this movement for the renewal of beauty in life to tread reverently, and to see to it that the blighting touch of the pedant and the expert is not laid upon it,' she said in dismissal of his claims.

Sharp and Neal were now running rival dance operations. Sharp had recruited Maud and Helen Karpeles, well-to-do sisters from north London who had attended the Stratford festival the previous summer, to his School of Morris. They had trained in order to teach the dance to the youngsters of the Mansfield House Settlement in Canning Town where they volunteered. In early 1910, they established a Folk Dance Club at the Portman Rooms in Baker Street; Sharp accompanied dancers on the piano.

On 4 May, the Esperance staged a performance at which many traditional dancers appeared. The press carried an interview with Mary the following day in which she said, 'I recognise no expert in Morris dancing, but the traditional dancer himself, and I recognise no expert teachers of Morris dancing but those who have been directly taught by the traditional dancer.' The press responded positively. *The Times* review referred to the traditional dancers as the experts and the *Morning Post* applauded Mary's desire to keep experts in their place. Francis Toye, music critic at *Vanity Fair*, asked why Sharp should award himself the position of expert and seek to excommunicate Mary and the Esperance. A battle of words was being played out in the press, and it was about to become crucial which of the two gained the ascendancy.

In addition to giving demonstration dances at the Stratford folk festival, Mary ran a vacation school for sixty teachers from London County Council schools at the Green Lady in Littlehampton in the spring of 1910. Florrie Warren taught the dancers and Clive Carey the songs. Seeing the success of the Green Lady classes, the governors of the Stratford festival suggested that an event dedicated to the teaching of dance be held there that August and that the school become an annual event. This was a huge opportunity. But who should run the school? As Mary and Cecil Sharp were unlikely to work together the directors would have to make a choice between them. The opportunity to establish an annual event drove the wedge further between Sharp, who needed to secure work, and Mary. The rivalry for the position of director of the Stratford summer school was now conducted by a heated public exchange. Sharp claimed that teaching should only be led by experts and 'accredited' teachers while Mary countered that the dances of 'unlettered folk' should be left in the hands of those also 'unlettered and ignorant of all technique'. Any person of average intelligence, she said, could teach a Morris dance, characterising the debates as one between pedants and those who were in touch with life itself.

Mary and Sharp fought for control of the Stratford summer school in a war of public letters. Sharp's dancers were now ready to perform in public. In May, the *Westminster Gazette* carried a piece designed to undermine Mary's authority, lamenting the radical defects in the Esperance dancers. In particular, Sharp selected for criticism the bent knee, the absence of ankle spring, and the lack of 'traditional dignity' that, he asserted, were the essential character of all genuine Morris dancing. Morris, he claimed, was a straight leg dance, whereas the Esperance dancers raised their thighs and moved their legs violently up and down 'after the manner of a high stepping horse'. Not only was the movement 'inelegant', but, he claimed, there was no traditional authority for such an up and down, rather than forward, movement. There is a suggestion of immodesty in his description of the female dancers. The girls were soon due to perform in Brussels and he sincerely hoped that before they went, they would take 'expert' supervision (presumably meaning himself) and do their best to cure their faults so that they might give their European neighbours a 'faithful exposition of our very beautiful native dance'. Sharp was now overtly calling the dance of the Esperance Guild 'inauthentic' and asserting that his standard was the one that should be imposed.

Mary fought back. She headed back to Headington with Clive Carey and Francis Toye to collect more dances for the repertoire; such collecting could also be expected to cement her reputation as an expert. In order to counter Sharp's criticisms, she consulted William Kimber about the authenticity of his interpretations of the dance and the key question as to whether the leg should be straight or bent at the knee. Since even Kimber himself could not trace his technique directly back over generations, his side having been revived after a hiatus, she concluded that there was no one accepted technique. She had, she wrote to Archibald Flower, the chair of trustees at the Stratford Birthplace Trust 'indubitably proved that the whole basis of Mr Sharp's contentions as an expert are entirely unfounded', which she found quite amusing. She returned to Stratford with Clive Carey and Florrie Warren in August to deliver a course of instruction to 200 enthusiasts who would go out into their communities and teach. She must have left Stratford confident that she would be invited to take the lead at the following year's dance school.

In October, the Esperance Morris Guild was offered use of Crosby Hall in Chelsea for monthly practice and Mary announced her intention of founding a national school. In November, she brought William Trafford of the Headington Quarrymen to London to teach. At 74, he had never been to the capital before and became separated from his chaperones and was lost on the Circle Line until located by a search party! Mary continued to combine her pursuit of the Morris with her pursuit of the vote, hosting an 'at home' for the WSPU in Newbury during one of her forays to Oxford. But there had been a hiatus in really militant activity for some months. Lady Constance's revelations about women's treatment in prison earlier in the year had coincided with a general election precipitated by the rejection of Lloyd George's 'pensions' budget by the House of Lords. Despite the misgivings of some supporters at the advantage that this might give to the Tory party, the WSPU had stuck to its policy of targeting Liberal candidates throughout the election campaign. The Liberal government was returned to power with a reduced majority. Campaigners hoped it would, therefore, be more open to negotiation on the issue of votes for women as it would be reliant on minor party support. Asquith had also conceded during the campaign that a women's suffrage amendment to any reform bill would not be subject to the party whip. Consequently, in the hope of progress, the WSPU had called a truce that – on account of unforeseen events – lasted the best part of a year.

Lady Constance's revelations about the treatment of women in prison had harmed the government and focused opinion, particularly amongst Members of Parliament; in the new session a Conciliation Committee, comprising members of all parties and from both houses, met to discuss the issue of votes for women. Lord Lytton, Lady Constance's brother, was in the chair. The committee proposed a bill which would give the vote to a limited number of female householders, though not on equal terms with men. The so-called Conciliation Bill was introduced to the Commons by a private member in June 1910. Over the course of the summer, numerous city and district councils passed resolutions in support of the bill, and when it passed a second reading with a large majority it seemed that the fight to win the vote was won. Had that been the case, it would have been in no small part due to the influence of the leaders of the Esperance. But there was not time for the bill to complete the Parliamentary process before the summer recess. The WSPU held fire again in the autumn, but the leadership did not trust Prime Minister Asquith and by November the mood had turned rebellious. On 10 November, Emmeline Pethick-Lawrence called on her audience at the Albert Hall to raise a £9,000 fighting fund; the target was achieved in an hour. In *Votes for Women*, Evelyn Sharp described Emmeline as 'the most remarkable treasurer in the world'. A week later, Asquith announced that stalemate had again been reached between the Commons and the Lords over Lloyd George's budget and that Parliament would once more be dissolved, leaving the women's suffrage bill out of time once more. No commitment as to its resurrection was made should the government be re-elected. It was the impact of this disappointment, together with the events of 'Black Friday', 18 November 1910, which precipitated the WSPU into all-out warfare.

This date is generally regarded as a turning point in suffragette attitudes to authority, pitching the WSPU into a sustained campaign of damage to property. In protest at the lack of any comment from the prime minister on the fate of the Conciliation Bill after the forthcoming election, Mrs Pankhurst and her supporters marched on Parliament. Aggressive policing saw many women injured as they tried to force their way through the cordon in a siege that lasted for hours. Members of the public stepped in to protect women from beatings and there were accusations of sexual assault. In anger and frustration, some women turned to window-breaking. It seemed to many that peaceable persuasion had failed, and, given the actions of the police on 18 November, was increasingly foolhardy. The campaign took its notorious turn towards property damage. Better to throw a stone and be arrested quickly, the women reasoned, than to march peacefully and risk a beating from the police. A few days later, 150 women were arrested for window-breaking after a deputation to Downing Street to protest at the treatment of women on 'Black Friday'. In *Votes for Women*, Emmeline declared that political change must come from revolution rather than evolution.

Though she was on the WSPU's national committee, Mary had other things on her mind. Having announced her intention to establish a national school, and still waiting on a decision from Stratford as to who should run the school of dance there the following year, she was unexpectedly offered the chance to take the dance revival international. Danish ballet dancer Adeline Genee had been sitting for her portrait with Neville Lytton when her attention was caught by some paintings he had done of Mary's Morris dancers. When Lytton sent her a ticket for an Esperance performance, Genee gave the ticket to an American friend named Emily Burbank who had been studying folk dance in Europe. Burbank was thrilled by what she saw and keen to establish a similar movement in the United States. She and an associate called at the offices of the Esperance Guild and invited Mary to initiate a Morris revival in America.

Mary departed by boat in December 1910, accompanied by Florrie Warren, for a four-month teaching tour. The pair would visit New York, Chicago, Boston and Philadelphia, as well as Toronto in Canada. For Florrie, a girl from the slums of St Pancras, the voyage must have been beyond imagination. Although no decision had been made as to who was to lead the programme at Stratford the following year, Mary saw the trip as an opportunity to promote the Stratford school and took announcements with her to drum up business in the United States. Advertising herself as Stratford's lead instructor gave her standing and her time teaching in America could be expected to give her an international reputation, enhancing her status as the leading light in the dance revival.

But Sharp's influence reached even to America. While Mary and Florrie were travelling, friends of his contacted her hosts. In an attempt to undermine her authority as a speaker and teacher it was claimed, incorrectly, that her methods had been rejected by the education authorities at home. Mary and Florrie arrived in a blizzard to find the streets of New York deep in snow and many of their engagements cancelled. But Mary was resourceful and Florrie gave their first demonstrations over the Christmas period. At the MacDowell Club she trained twenty-four dancers for a Christmas masque. One of the New York papers declared:

> There is certainly no more fascinating exposition of the origin, development, and aims of the movement than that Miss Neal can give, and the stock of stories she has gathered in her long work among the girls who hail her affectionately as 'Sister Mary', would humanize a lecture on a far less inspiring subject than folk dancing.

Mary and Florrie spent a week in each district of the cities they visited, teaching 'Step and Fetch Her', 'Blue-eyed Stranger', 'Rakers of Mallow', 'Sally Luker', and the 'Lively Jig' to groups of thirty-six pupils. 'We have had a wonderful reception,' Mary wrote in her account of this trip in her introduction to the second Esperance Morris book, 'and are already at work training a number of school teachers who bid fair to rival our English dancers. They will illustrate lectures and help us in our entertainments.'

In Boston they taught Harvard students, and at Columbia a group from the Sons and Daughters of the Revolution. They spoke at high schools, women's clubs, societies and universities. Once taught, the pupils would be able to hand on the dances as the Esperance girls had done in England. In Toronto, the pair reconnected with a Morris team of boys from Newbury in Berkshire who had learned the dance with Esperance teachers and who had emigrated to Canada where they were now passing on the dances. They also met old members of the Esperance Club who had founded a similar organisation to that of their youth in St Pancras.

Florrie Warren was no ordinary dancer. A girl of remarkable talent, she charmed American audiences and was invited to dance at Carnegie Hall. Then the unexpected happened. At a tea party in their honour in Boston, Florrie met a young lawyer named Arthur Brown. Three months later, as Florrie and Mary prepared to sail to England, Brown jumped aboard the ship and proposed. Mary returned home alone. Florrie remained in the United States, taking teaching engagements until she and Arthur Brown were married.

On Mary's return to England, she found that Sharp had used her lengthy absence networking, writing to the press, adding to his collection of dances and lobbying the Stratford organisers to appoint him and his dancers to provide the teaching and demonstrations at the following years' events, rather than Mary and the Esperance Guild. Mary now considered her old collaborator to be obsessed with tradition and an 'accuracy' that she believed to be spurious and impossible to pin down, at the expense of the 'spirit' of the dance. Rather than pinning down the detail of every movement, she allowed her dancers freedom of expression within the set steps and moves. She regarded his desire to pin down the dances to a form performed at one moment in time as absurd. She had collected many dances herself and her teachers had been instructed by traditional dancers; she argued that no two sides performed a dance in the same way or any one side the same way on two separate occasions. Nor did any two men perform their steps in the same way. For her, the dance was a living, evolving thing – not a thing to be constrained. And she believed that there had always been freedom within the traditional dances. A folk dance, she told the American *Musical Herald*, unlike a folk song, was not something that had been composed but something that evolved in performance. The argument was as much about ownership and power as academic authenticity. Sharp sought to pin down and categorise, to own and control the dance, like an explorer naming, defining and claiming new territory. Mary saw her role as understanding and celebrating the dance and the dancers. She wanted to get people of all classes dancing and reconnecting with their heritage. Her priority was not to preserve the dance of the late nineteenth century in aspic but to embrace its possibilities for effecting social change in the twentieth.

In February 1911 – whilst Mary was still in the United States – the WSPU's honorary secretary, Mabel Tuke, took the Esperance Guild to Oxford to dance a programme with the Headington Quarrymen, whose members had taught them the first dances five years earlier. The *Oxford Journal* billed the event as a unique opportunity to see the original instructors and 'those who are responsible for its spread through the kingdom'. The presence of the Headington men demonstrated that the Esperance dancers were no interlopers and that the Esperance Guild was rooted in the traditional dance movement. The grand reunion of dancers at the Masonic Hall was a creative collaboration between a group of rural men who had preserved the traditions of the dance and the urban women who were campaigning for their enfranchisement. Mabel Tuke was accompanied by May Start and by Clive Carey who performed songs; the Quarrymen were accompanied by Mark Cox, a fiddler who had visited the Esperance in London, and William Trafford. The *Westminster Gazette* contrasted the bucolic Headington men, with the town-bred girls: 'Clearly it was serious business to the Headington men. Not a smile, even for a second, touched their compressed lips … it was as though half a dozen elephants had solemnly and in a dignified manner decided to indulge in a few capers.' When the Esperance danced the same dances, it was different, claimed the reporter, for to follow the men slavishly would have been an odd parody. The effect of the afternoon was to impress the audience with the innate adaptability of the Morris, 'which is still the time-worn heritage of the soil, but which, transplanted from the village green to the London street, acquires a new vigour and a new motive'. Mary would surely have approved this interpretation, which did not dwell on 'inauthentic' departures from the exact style of the Headington side but celebrated the vitality and adaptability of the Morris. Indeed, the writer's summing has all the hallmarks of Mary's vision: 'And hidden away in the heart of many a townsman is the ancient original influence of the green fields and the open sky, which causes him, maybe, to skip so easily into the Morris when some enthusiastic revivalist brings it his way'. The account of the event in the *Oxford Journal* has clearly been taken directly from a piece written by Mary, or someone whose vision was very close to hers, with its emphasis on the meaning of the dance to the culturally disenfranchised dancers: 'Only those who have witnessed a performance like this can realise what this giving back of the Morris dance has meant for England. It has given to the inarticulate a means of self-expression and added the priceless pleasure that comes from the practice of an art.'

The Oxford Journal reported that the Esperance was experiencing a demand for instructors that it was unable to meet and stressed the rigour of Mary's methods – with a subtle dig at Sharp and his propensity for seeing transmission of the dance as being as simple as transmission of a song:

> The difference between the learning of a folk song and of a Morris dance is that the one can be got

from a book, while the other must be taught by word of mouth ... It is difficult to over-estimate the importance of this direct oral teaching. Without it not only would there be a break in the 'direct succession' from traditional dancers, but there is the danger of intentional modifications creeping in and completely altering the spirit of the dance.

Far from suggesting that what Mary teaches is inauthentic, more concerned with political ends than purity, the article proposes that by learning from a book 'modifications' might creep in, meaning that Sharp's versions of the dances may be less authentic than hers. And, the writer adds: 'the Morris is a country dance, full of vigour and smelling of the fields. It is totally unsuited for producing the subtler effects of the ballroom'. Mary had once recounted an old sailor – himself a Morris dancer – watching the Esperance and telling her, 'That is the dancing my heart, it's clean dancing, and I would not have missed the sight for two big apples.' Others – and by implication Sharp – her proxy seems to suggest, are guilty of modifying and gentrifying the dance. This insistence on the authenticity of the dances as taught by the Esperance girls is one that Mary went on to stress in *English Folk-Song and Dance* which she published in 1915 with Frank Kidson:

I have kept very carefully to the traditional lines, make a great point of having those whom I send out to teach taught by country dancers without the intervention of professional dance instructors, so that today, after eight years practice, I believe they are dancing as much like the original dancers as is possible.

Sharp was claiming respect for the folk dance tradition from the urban middle and upper classes. And in doing so, he was codifying it and introducing rules, judging what could and could not be part of the official canon. But the dance movement at the beginning of the twentieth century was a revival, and a revival of something that had never had rules in the first place. In *English Folk-Song and Dance* Mary explained that in recording the dances it had always been necessary to decide on the most typical step seen in the traditional dancers and to adopt it. But she recognised that any two people might feel different interpretations amongst the dancers were the most 'typical'. For her though, the key characteristics were vigour and virility and she scoffed at the 'pointed toe of ordinary ball room and stage dances' that had crept in, in what appears to have been a jibe at Sharp's gentrification. Instead, she gave an impassioned defence of her style and of the girls who had learned their steps from illiterate Morris men, not from a professional dancer with a vocabulary of technical terms: 'They love the dance, and it is always encored when we give it in public.' The book is her retrospective manifesto. She asks:

What, then, is the natural way for these ever changing, ever evolving dances to be passed on? I unhesitatingly say that they should be learnt in the first instance from the traditional dancer and passed on in the same way. The written instructions are only useful as a reminder of steps and evolutions and should never be made an unalterable and fixed standard. For if folk dancing has been evolving through all these countless generations, who shall fix the exact moment when evolution ceased and the steps and evolutions became fixed and unalterable? So are, as I have seen, traditional dancers; I have noticed that not only does every side in every village dance a little differently, but each man has his own way with the steps, and still further, the same man may dance differently every time he does the dance. I am behind no one in the desire that these dances shall be as accurately transcribed and as carefully taught as possible, and that the general character and atmosphere shall be preserved, but it is just because of this desire that I would have the dances as far as possible left to the interpretation of those who are unhampered by technical knowledge and unconfined by technical terms and academic restrictions.

Hers is a cry to trust in the instincts and skills and culture of working people – both the Morris men and the slum girls – a plea against turning the Morris into something middle class that can be adjudicated on only by leisured 'experts' who would nit-pick and claim to know more than those who had learned the dances from their remaining practitioners. In a plea for the joy of the dance to be accessible to all, she asserts that all that is needed to pass on a dance is a series of demonstrations:

There seems to be in these traditional dance movements something natural and inevitable, so that it is more easy to dance them correctly than to do them wrongly, and I think it is in this spirit that they should be taught. There is nothing strained and difficult, nothing artificial or exotic; all is simple, dignified, vigorous and joyful.

Mary claimed the dance for all: 'While all dance correctly, each dances a little differently from the others. Nothing is less to be desired that that any school or any individual should take possession of this national treasure.' Looking back in 1915 she rather regretted that the dance had become officially recognised as part of school curriculum, with the necessity of books of instruction which had led inevitably to codification and greater emphasis on correct exposition than on the joy of the dance. 'I would rather the dances had remained in the memories of dancers.'

Physically, in the United States, and in print, Mary was fighting for her vision. While she was away, a history of the Shakespeare festival had been published. *The Shakespeare Revival and the Stratford-upon-Avon Movement* by Reginald Buckley contained a chapter by Mary on Folk-art. In it, she presents a history of the folk revival – in dance, song, plays and games. Attempting to shape the narrative of the revival to reflect her own political vision, she claims that the folk revival has its roots in the movement for social change. The first seeds of the movement, she claims, were sown amongst 'the people' not by wealthy song collectors, but by the city settlements such as the Mission where she and Emmeline had met. The modern folk movement, in her narrative, begins as 'a protest against the conditions which gave to one class all the opportunities of enjoying the beautiful things in life'. She recounts her own history and that of Emmeline:

> A dawning consciousness that it was true of all classes that man could not live by bread alone sent a band of men and women into the poorest districts of London to share as far as it was possible the advantages which leisure and education had given them with those who had been deprived of their birth-right of joy and beauty.

In such settlements, men and women of all classes came together and the demands of the workers for a fuller life was met by those who were ready to meet that demand. Music, dance, painting and drama were brought within reach of working people. And, she asserts, those middle-class people who went to give, found themselves in receipt of insight into the deeper truths of life 'unknown to those who study only books'. In Mary's narrative, the folk revival was not a result of the efforts of collectors like Sharp (though she does not name him) but 'of this meeting of human fellowship of all classes and all conditions'. It is her claim that the folk revival had been radical from the outset.

The story of the Esperance fits neatly into this narrative; the dance had been taken up and spread nationwide by a club for working girls whose objects were to enable them to enjoy cultural experiences to which they would otherwise have had no access. And Mary speculated that they were particularly suited to the task as 'ancestral memory' enabled the girls to learn the dances easily, making them natural interpreters and teachers of the dance of other 'unlettered folk'. Her 'ancestral memory' theory may have no scientific basis, but in practical terms she was rejecting the notion that the practice of folk dance needs special training or that its teachers required a vocabulary of technical terms, asserting instead that it is a natural expression of joy and an organic thing that must grow and develop: 'The dance of to-day will change tomorrow if it still expresses the genuine emotion of tomorrow.' Mary resisted the dance being taken away from her girls by 'experts' and made intellectual and middle class, imbued with arcane expertise and complicated technical terms.

Mary set out her case eloquently in the performance of her dancers and in print. But Cecil Sharp had used her absence to stake his claim to be the leading expert on folk dance. The Karpeles sisters' folk club in Baker Street had grown in popularity; one fundraising concert at which Sharp spoke attracted an audience of 500 wealthy people. It was an audience that he was keen to cultivate. He was also cultivating Archibald Flower, chairman of the trustees of Shakespeare's Birthplace Trust, and lobbying for the position of director of the dance summer school. Despite having come relatively late to the dance, he had certain advantages in his favour. He had a musical background and connections with London's professional musical elite; Gustav Holst had dedicated his *Somerset Rhapsody* (which incorporated folk tunes) to Sharp, and he was an associate of the composers and folk song collectors Ralph Vaughan Williams and George Butterworth.

Mary's networking connections were amongst activists and campaigners, not necessarily useful in supporting her case to those who would make the decision at Stratford. That she was also involved in a radical campaign of civil disobedience only compounded that disadvantage. Sharp was dealing with men in positions of authority from his own social and professional milieu. Edward Burrows, the Sussex inspector of schools, had introduced him to Edmond Holmes, the educationalist and chief inspector of schools, shortly before the decision to include folk dance in school curricula. Though Mary had a track record as a teacher and was building a reputation as a collector, it was difficult, in a society where women were not even allowed to take degrees from Britain's most prestigious universities, for a woman to challenge the expertise and authority of a man of Sharp's professional musical training and social standing.

Mary believed that Archibald Flower was committed to holding a conference to publicly debate the contested issues before any decision about the coming Stratford summer school was made. But in May 1911 the organisers of the Shakespeare folk festival appointed Cecil Sharp to the post of director of the programme. Mary was asked to remain in the unpaid role of honorary secretary to the festival. Sharp could not have been surprised when she refused to undertake the organisation and administration while leaving all crucial artistic decisions involving the dance school to him. She resigned from the festival committee. Though Sharp commented disdainfully that she had 'rejected any olive branch offered', he must have been privately pleased at her withdrawal which left him with a free hand. For Mary, it must have been a bitter disappointment to find herself edged out of the school at which her girls had demonstrated and taught so successfully only a year previously.

Notwithstanding the Stratford decision, the Esperance dancers remained in great demand. In May 1911, Mary and Clive Carey directed their performances at the great Festival of Empire at Crystal Palace. Blanche Payling was dispatched to teach at Thaxted in Essex at the invitation of the town's 'Red Vicar', Conrad Noel. She taught three classes a day there and returned with Mary later in the year to see sixty children dancing in the town flower show. There was even talk of sending dancers to India, Mary told the Women's Imperial Health Congress at Caxton Hall in July, as the authorities in Baroda (now Vadodara) had invited dancers to introduce the dances there. While Sharp taught at the Stratford summer school with the Karpeles sisters, Mary and Carey set out to collect new dances in Yorkshire. There they met the Flamborough Sword dancers and invited them to give a public performance at Crosby Hall. Mary made plans to hold an Easter dance school at the Green Lady in future years, but she remained bitter at the loss of the teaching position at Stratford and her comments in programmes and press articles continued to argue against the need for experts to interpose themselves between those who knew the dances and those who wished to learn them.

On 15 September, *Votes for Women* published a long article by the WSPU's secretary, Mabel Tuke, on the spread of the Morris revival across the country. Like Mary, Mabel allied the dance with the fight for the vote and the social revolution that she and fellow progressive women believed they were bringing about. She told followers:

> It stands for a readjustment of current philosophies about life, a revolution as real as ever was achieved in the past, not by sword and bloodshed and strife, but through the medium of dance and song, the spirit of a merry heart, the rousing of the countryside and the village, and the weaving about our crowded towns and cities of the 'impossible dream'.

The dance was being woven into the pageantry of the suffragette movement, contributing another facet to the vision of joy and hope that attracted supporters to the political campaign.

In particular, Mabel celebrated her fellow committee member:

> In the forefront of those practical visionaries who are spending all their energies and lavishing an endless thought and love upon this peaceful revolution stands the vivid and magnetic personality of Miss Mary Neal, its protagonist and leader. No dry bones can resist the spirit which she breathes with such courage and vitality, and her life's work on behalf of the working girls of the Esperance Club is crowned by the formation of the Guild for the Revival of Folk and Morris Dancing, with which her name has been of late years more specially connected, and in which she has taken so prominent a share.

Mabel's words are typical of the reverence accorded the suffragette leaders by their followers:

> No stultifying pessimism can possibly live in its atmosphere of radiant hopefulness, and the best advice one can offer to weary misanthropes convinced that the future holds nothing but gloom and desolation for themselves and the world at large would be to insist that they should accompany you to the next performance of the Esperance Guild. The deadening load of dull depression would slip away by the end of the evening, and in its place something of a sense of fun and frolic, memories of childhood's innocent days, of green fields and blue skies, would come back, and the tender springs of an altogether human emotion might even well up in the dry wilderness which for long had taken hold of a heart.

Mabel had travelled the country with the youngsters and called their efforts 'merrymaking adventures'. Like Mary, she saw the dance as a harbinger of a future which harked back to an imagined past idyll that had been destroyed by modern life:

> They are the heralds and prophets of a gospel new and yet old, which the fever of modern industrial life has almost succeeded in destroying. They stand for the re-affirmation ... of the truth that man cannot live by bread alone, that love and childlikeness, happiness and healthy merriment are the foods of the perfect

physical body, as well as the inspiration and life of the soul, and they bring with them such a contagion of mirth and so irresistible an appeal that I can always win a ready and enthusiastic response.

And like Mary, she claimed something eternal, beyond and before organised Christianity to the dance:

Pan, the nature god of old, must have touched their twinkling feet and breathed into them something of his way who made the ancient days ring to his tune, for the irresistible frolic and lighthearted footing of the Morris dancers, the exquisite plaintive beauty of some folk song melody, and the fascinating unselfconscious charm of the singing games will rouse even the most blasé of onlookers, transporting them in spirit to the very far off land they had fancied gone for ever, where the old earth smiles always happily upon her children, the air is rapturous with the singing of birds and the golden sunshine is over all.

Mabel Tuke looked to the lost rural past in a vision for the future of the nation using the somewhat stilted language of the poetry of a previous age:

The Utopian is a great believer in village greens and the maypole. England is to be less stiff and less self-conscious. She is to dance and sing from pure lightness of heart, and in the open air, upon green grass, and beneath the blue sky. The Utopians, in their visions of a future of England, always see the young men and graceful sunburnt girls footing it upon the turf, and banks of merry children playing games which are actually childlike and simple ... Who would not confess with pride and joy to such a dream as this!

Mary had now returned to active campaigning for the vote. In October 1911, she was in Leeds, opening the WSPU's offices there in readiness for a municipal election campaign. Despite the anger generated by 'Black Friday' in November the previous year and frustration at the general election that had disappointed hopes of a bill being promoted by government, the WSPU's truce held into 1911, even when a revived Conciliation Bill was dismissed after two readings for lack of time. The Chancellor of the Exchequer, David Lloyd George, had assured Lord Lytton that the government would allot time to the completion of the bill's passing in the autumn session of Parliament and Asquith had confirmed that the assurance would be honoured. Once again, it appeared that battle for the vote had been won. The WSPU held its truce throughout the summer of 1911 and the celebrations for the coronation of George V in June. On 17 June, a glorious pageant of women, militant and non-militant, had processed through London in the hope and belief that a new reign and a new session of Parliament would at last see a women's suffrage bill becoming law. Mrs Pankhurst and Emmeline had marched at its head, dressed in white; Mabel Tuke had followed with Christabel Pankhurst. Every suffrage-supporting group was represented on the march to the Albert Hall, including the Esperance. 'That I should have been present on the day of your assured triumph will always remain one of the permanent joys of my existence,' wrote the journalist Henry Nevinson, while his colleague W.T. Stead celebrated 'the redoubtable trio' who had engineered the movement: 'the Pankhursts *mere et fille* and Mrs Pethick-Lawrence'. The atmosphere on the stage was celebratory. It was a bitter disappointment, therefore, when, on Parliament reconvening in the autumn, Asquith announced that he proposed, not the resurrection of the Conciliation Bill, but a government-sponsored suffrage bill for men. He held out only the hope that an amendment might be brought in include women.

Mrs Pankhurst was away on a tour of the United States when this announcement was made. It fell to Emmeline Pethick-Lawrence to convene a large meeting at the Albert Hall where she appealed to the women's self-respect. 'I would rather die than submit to such humiliation,' she said, before reading out a telegram from Mrs Pankhurst. The truce was over. 'We meet tonight, a united army on the eve of battle.' By killing the cross-party Conciliation Bill and bringing in a bill to extend the vote to more men, Emmeline told her supporters, Lloyd George had turned reform of the franchise into a party issue, dividing the Liberal and Conservative pro-suffrage alliance that had supported the Conciliation Bill. She accused the government of deceiving women as to its intentions in order to stage a peaceful coronation undisrupted by militant action, and then betraying their trust. When she led a deputation to the prime minister the following day, she was accompanied by Esperance supporters Mabel Tuke and Lady Constance, as well as Christabel and Sylvia Pankhurst and leaders of the WFL and NUWSS. The atmosphere within the WSPU, Emmeline later recalled, was 'white hot'. After the meeting with Asquith, she led another deputation to the Houses of Parliament on 21 November where she was arrested. A coordinated attack on windows in Whitehall took place the same evening, during which 200 women were arrested. Emmeline's husband stood bail for 175 of them. Pointing out that men who had fought successfully for the vote in the past had done far worse, Emmeline told her supporters that, 'Those who suggest that men may fight for their freedom but women must fawn and cringe and avoid any unladylike resistance are well-meaning but stupid.'

Mary's continued membership of the WSPU's national committee and support for Emmeline and her leadership was an aggravating factor in her inability to find common ground with Sharp. She may never have thrown a stone, but she made no move to disassociate herself from the assaults on property that were now a stock-in-trade of the organisation on whose national committee she sat. Neither did Mabel Tuke or Lady Constance. She was still smarting at the decision to appoint Sharp director at Stratford and complained to Flower that the selection had not been conducted as she would have expected; there had been no public discussion of their differing positions or suitability. And she continued to lobby for the Esperance Guild, comparing its effectiveness with that of Sharp's new Folk Dance Society. The Stratford organisers, she suggested, were backing the wrong horse in terms of social and geographical reach:

> After six years drudging away I am now satisfied with the progress we are making. We had 550 pupils in November, mostly in the north. The new Folk Dance Society deceives no one … Stratford is merely making a corner in Folk Dances for a select few while the really national movement grows apace.

Mary attended a dance event promoted by Cecil Sharp at Kensington Town Hall on 1 December. She took notes during the performance, presumably alerting Sharp to the fact that she intended to write a review. Her account appeared in *The Observer* the following Sunday. 'The atmosphere, the movements, the general style of the dancing is not that inspired by the peasant mind, the uncultured, unlettered artist of the field,' she told readers, 'It is rather the adaptation of this by the cultured musician.' She dismissed Sharp's rigorous accuracy as representing no more than what a 'cultured' man thought the dance ought to be, whereas the 'authentic' peasant dancers displayed something more elemental as they 'danced in a sort of trance, in a mood inarticulate, unselfconscious; each man had his own way with the steps, no two dancing precisely alike, and yet the same mood was so heavy upon all that the general effect was harmonious and curiously impressive'.

Sharp had now totally disassociated himself from her, founding his own national society to much fanfare in the papers. The Karpeles sisters dissolved their dance club and joined him. The English Folk Dance Society would fulfil the proposed remit for a national society set out three years earlier at the Goupil conference. With an executive committee made up of people of his own choosing, Sharp would be able to dictate policy and direct operations without negotiating terms with Mary or any of her supporters.

May Start (1882–1957)

Another young working-class woman who was drawn into the campaign for the vote through Mary, Emmeline and the Esperance was May Start. May began life in the London millinery trade and went to work for Fred and Emmeline as a teenager in 1901. In 1906, she was one of the early Esperance dancers, performing in Maidenhead. She taught games to the Esperance children, accompanied them to dance events, and became Emmeline and Fred's housekeeper, responsible for the practicalities of life in their London and country homes. After 1910, when hunger strikes became a feature of the campaign for the vote, May was charged with taking care of recuperating suffragettes in Surrey. Like her employer, May declined to take part in the census of 1911 in protest, refusing to give her details to the enumerator.

May married Wilfred Walter in 1925 and took the surname Start-Walter. She remained close to Mary Neal and the Pethick-Lawrences for the rest of their lives.

Mabel Tuke (1871–1962)

Mabel Tuke was another of Emmeline Pethick-Lawrence's contacts who came to the campaign for the vote via the Esperance Club and also played a part in the Morris revival. Born Mabel Kate Lear, and affectionately known as 'Pansy', she grew up in Woolwich where her father was a surveyor with the Royal Engineers. In 1905, she was in mourning for the death of her husband – who had died of a fever in South Africa – when she met Emmeline on board the ship taking them both back to England. Emmeline recruited her into volunteering with the Esperance Club and when Emmeline became treasurer of the WSPU's London committee shortly afterwards, Mabel took the position of secretary.

Working with Emmeline, Mary Neal and the Pankhursts, Mabel Tuke was central to the leadership of the militant movement, and closely supported Emmeline, taking care of her Surrey house while Emmeline was in prison and nursing other campaigners there. Mary Gawthorpe wrote that 'there was something velvety about Pansy. She was a great asset to Mrs Pethick-Lawrence. I have noticed her counterpart in other movements. Those treasures happier in the comparative background help the leader on a dozen fronts at once.'

Mabel Tuke seldom took radical action herself, though in 1912 she served three weeks for throwing a stone through the window of 10 Downing Street. After a mass window-breaking session by supporters she was charged, alongside Fred, Emmeline and Mrs Pankhurst, with conspiracy to commit criminal damage, though charges against her were later dropped.

After the split between the Pankhursts and the Pethick-Lawrences, Mabel remained with the WSPU, often travelling to take instructions from Christabel Pankhurst in Paris. In the 1920s, she established a short-lived tea shop with the Pankhursts in the south of France, supplying most of the funding and undertaking the baking.

Mabel Tuke volunteered with the Esperance until the outbreak of the First World War. She collected dances from the men of Abingdon, and in early 1911 she and Emmeline's housekeeper, May Start, accompanied the Esperance dancers to Oxford while Mary was travelling in the United States. Later that year she penned a long article for *Votes for Women* entitled 'The Magic of the Morris' in which she drew connections between the Morris dance, the militant suffragette movement and Mary and Emmeline's 'impossible dream' of a transformed society. The Morris revival, she said, was 'racing at express speed throughout the length and breadth of England ... Impossible and fantastic it may appear to some', she wrote, 'nevertheless our dream materialises, we see it incarnate here and now'.

In the pages of *Votes for Women*, whose cause would seem to have little obviously in common with the objects of the dance revival, Mabel Tuke wove the aspirations of the Esperance for a more equal and transformed society with the political demands of the WSPU. She also took the opportunity to assert Mary's place in leading the dance revolution to her readership of militant-supporting women. For Mabel, as for Mary, the dance revival provided a vision of a revived country for which they, and suffragettes of a similar political outlook, saw themselves as fighting.

Nellie Chaplin (1858–1930)

Nellie Chaplin was one of the many people involved in the folk music revival who were drawn into the feud between Mary Neal and Cecil Sharp.

Nellie was a highly talented pianist. She trained in London and Hamburg and played piano on the concert stage, both as a soloist and with her sisters Kate and Mabel as part of the Chaplin Trio. British orchestras were closed to women (other than harpists) until the First World War so forming quartets and quintets with other women was the only means for female performers to make a living. Critics, however, tended to judge them as 'lady' players and treat them as a curiosity rather than taking their talent and skills seriously.

The Chaplin Trio played a traditional 'Romantic' and contemporary repertoire in venues across the country and abroad, but in about 1900 they began to revive Baroque and Elizabethan pieces. Nellie took up the harpsichord and her sisters explored early string instruments. Much of this music had been written to be danced to and Nellie began to explore volumes of early country and courtly dances and to present them alongside the music. The mix of early music and dance was popular with audiences.

In 1907, independently of Cecil Sharp and Mary Neal, Nellie Chaplin began to offer classes in country dancing at the Hampstead Conservatoire. She came to the initiative as a musician rather than a dancer, curious about the interplay between dance and music, and advocated that music students should learn the dances that had once accompanied the music that they were performing in order to understand its rhythms.

Chaplin encountered *The English Dancing Master: or Plaine and easie Rules for the Dancing of Country Dances, with the Tune to each Dance* at the British Library. It had been published by John Playford in London in 1651 for an audience of well-to-do people. She published three volumes of dances from this collection, studying the steps and figures before incorporating them into the Trio's performance repertoire. But, as Mary Neal, she found her scholarship dismissed. Far from welcoming Chaplin's research, Cecil Sharp commented that the dances of village greens and village fairs had been corrupted by publication in Playford's volume for use in parlours and drawing rooms. Despite Playford's collection being evidence of how dances were performed 250 years earlier, Cecil

Sharp dismissed their relevance, seeing the 'authentic' dances as those of the countryside and working people. The dancing masters of the wealthy had manipulated the Playford dances, he said, so that they were not 'not pure folk dances'.

Chaplin's intent was never to 'accurately' represent how the dances might have been danced, either by the well-to-do seventeenth-century purchasers of Playford's volume or their country predecessors a century or more earlier, or to adjudicate on which era's interpretation was most 'authentic', but to entertain her audiences and to introduce them to seventeenth-century music. Nonetheless, she was caught in the crossfire of Sharp's feud with Mary Neal when some of Mary's students danced in one of her concerts. Sharp disparaged her teaching and described her Blackpool music festival as representing 'the worst type of Chaplin come Esperance dancing'.

Chapter Six

A Split in the Ranks 1912

Though Sharp had won the battle for Stratford, the battle for influence across the country was not settled and neither was the question of the vote for women. Early in 1912, J. Curwen & Sons published the second *Esperance Morris Book*, a collection of Morris dances, country dances, sword dances and sea shanties. It was a collaborative effort by Mary, Clive Carey, the conductor Geoffrey Toye and Florrie Warren; the poet John Masefield, also a contributor to *Votes for Women*, granted permission for the use of words to some of the sea shanties. Mary dedicated the book to 'the traditional dancers of England, in whose memory there still linger the dances and melodies of long ago, and who have made possible that joyous revival of the folk dance from which we hope so much for the children of England'. It can be seen as Mary's manifesto. In the introduction – written while she was in the United States and in response to Sharp having written her out of the second edition of *The Book of Morris* – she laid claim to her place in the history of the dance and the Esperance girls' direct connection with the surviving traditional dancers:

The story of the origin of the revival of the Morris dance, and the unique part taken in that revival by the members of the Esperance Club, needs no re-telling today. It is, perhaps, not so generally known that until after the official sanction of the Morris dance by the Board of Education and its inclusion in the school curriculum, the instructors sent out by the Esperance Club were the only ones who had been directly taught by country dancers, and that they – and they only – had up till that time carried the dances throughout the length and breadth of England.

Having claimed the Esperance's place in history, she set out her vision for the future:

> As time goes on I am more and more convinced that if the movement for the restoration of English folk dance to its natural inheritors, the folk, is to continue to be a success, every care must be taken to preserve the simple and joyous spirit with which its first interpreters are identified. These dances, danced in the open, were expressive of the most primitive emotions.

Once again, she asserted that the Morris was the dance of ordinary people and its spirit the spirit of ordinary folk. Influenced by the anthropologist Sir James Frazer and his popular theories about ancient tradition she piled meaning on to speculation about the origins of the dance:

> In the days when they were part of the national life they were danced at lamb sales, midsummer fairs, Whitsuntide festivals, and as part of mummers' plays.

In all this there are indications that in the days prior to the Christian era they were part of ancient religious ceremonial. I lately paid another visit to Abingdon from which place three dances from volume 1 were collected, and noted that the horns carried in the dance ... were tipped with gold.

This, she claimed, indicated the sacred or sacrificial beast and was proof of the religious origin of the dances. She read significance into the fact that the dances which she and Mabel Tuke had collected at Abingdon end in a circle, as one of the Headington dances, 'Bean Setting', begins with a circle and surmised that both indicate a ceremonial meaning connected with the worship of the sun. She even went as far as reading vestiges of virgin sacrifice into Morris traditions performed at Kirtlington in Oxfordshire.

Some of these assertions may seem absurd, but at the heart of her challenge to Sharp is a deep respect for the villagers from whom she has collected the dances and a belief that their dances should not be turned into something requiring technical expertise:

When one has been in these remote old-world villages and talked to the old, old folk in whose memory, even when too old to dance, there still lingers the tradition of the dance and the customs associated with it one realises more and more how important it is to keep the atmosphere of this revival as it used to be. Some of the traditional dancers can neither read nor write,

they are simple, unlettered folk, and so no learning,
no scholarly training, no technical skill in music or
in ordinary dancing is necessary either to learn or to
teach these natural peasant dances.

Not only is a high degree of literacy not needed to learn the
dances, but they have a quality that simply cannot be taught by
book learning. These simple people would find Sharp's works
beyond their comprehension: 'I wonder sometimes how the
attitude of mind … of some of the present-day exponents of
the dances would appear to these simple and sincere peasant
minds.' Finally, she expressed her fear of the spirit of the dance
being crushed by adoption in schools using Sharp's methods
and questioned whether, after all, it might not have been better
had the dance never been added to the curriculum:

[I]f the learning and teaching of these dances is to be
to either teacher or pupil an added burden, merely an
extra school task, it had been better that these dances
had never been re-discovered. On the contrary, there
should be in these dances something which sets free
the spirit, something which so adds to the joy of life, so
energises and vitalizes every other part of the school
work that it will be more easily and better done.

Just about everything in Mary's introduction is an answer to
Sharp and a refutation of his claims. She stresses the simple
and the joyful, that the dances belong outside, not in classroom
or library, and that the 'unlettered' somehow 'own' them, and

she emphasises the care she has always taken to note the dances from traditional dancers, explaining that William Kimber had not been in the original Headington side but had joined after its revival, so his steps differed from many old members of the original side. The Esperance, she thereby claims, have gone back further than Sharp. She embraces the term 'merry' that had so upset him, assuring readers that, 'the merry Morris still lives in the hearts of the English people.' And she announces plans for the Esperance Guild to establish classes in the manufacturing centres of Manchester and Leeds in addition to the August summer school at Littlehampton.

The second introduction by the assistant editor of the *Westminster Gazette*, Philip Macer Wright, builds on Mary's theme, setting out a Utopian vision of the Esperance as a Guild of National Joy leading a revolution on village greens. 'England is to be less stiff and less self-conscious. She is to dance and sing from pure lightness of heart and in the open air, upon green grass and beneath the blue sky.' He envisages 'lithe young men and graceful sunburned girls footing it upon the turf, and bands of merry children playing games'. But what is radical about his vision is not his claim that the dancers' kinship with Mother Earth has remained intact through all the vicissitudes of slum life, but his claim that it is these London dancers who best represent Englishness, not the children of the wealthy or the babies of duchesses, but the 'common children, from mean streets'. And these youngsters are prophets, showing those who watch them 'a promised land in which the child shall be paramount, a land in which the lives of children shall be singing games'. It is a radical vision, of the essence of Englishness rooted in the poor and the disinherited rather than in the refined, and of future childhoods free of poverty, degradation and labour. It is Mary's 'impossible dream' being foreshadowed in the dance.

While Mary was speaking at suffrage meetings and setting out her vision for society, however, Cecil Sharp was consolidating his position as the authority on the Morris dance. In addition to the four-week long programme training teachers at Stratford, he had built up a busy schedule of lectures and performances by his Chelsea dancers. He had formed a national society, and he had begun to widen his remit to collect the sword dances of the north of England, carols, and other folk traditions. His dance repertoire was outgrowing Mary's and he was networking with supporters. But as he travelled the country, he found plenty of support for her vision. He found Sunderland to be 'a hot bed of Nealism' and complained in February 1912 of being 'attacked on all sides'. The teachers at Stratford were not completely on board with his style and methods either and made their feelings known. Justifying himself to Archibald Flower, he blamed Mary for the discord: 'If the teachers round you are incensed with me it is not from anything that I have said to them but because their minds have been poisoned against me by my enemies.'

Despite these setbacks for Sharp, in effect Mary had now been ousted from the movement she had initiated and done so much to promote. Emmeline was about to suffer a similar fate. On the night of 5 March 1912, she and Fred were arrested at the WSPU's offices and charged with conspiracy to commit criminal damage, being held responsible for the

mass stone-throwing incidences the previous year. Mabel Tuke
– already in prison for another offence – and Mrs Pankhurst
were charged with the same offence. Sharp's sister Evelyn
happened to call into the WSPU's offices as the arresting police
officers arrived. Before he was hand-cuffed, Fred handed her
a cheque transferring the WSPU's funds into the account of
physicist Hertha Ayrton. He also asked her to take over the
running of *Votes for Women* in his absence. He and Emmeline
were then taken to Bow Street police station where they
remained overnight. Christabel Pankhurst was away from the
office; tipped off by Evelyn, she fled to Paris. Her whereabouts
were not revealed for months, requiring the police to follow up
reports of sightings all over the country.

Unaware of what was taking place at Clement's Inn, Mary
was awoken by the police; Emmeline had asked that she call at
the couple's apartment to fetch nightwear and bring it to the
cells. Unable to find a siphon of soda water for Fred, Mary
called at the Savoy Hotel on her way. She was barred from
entry when the taxi-driver mentioned where she was headed
but the management had a siphon brought out to her. When
she reached the cells at Bow Street, Fred handed her a cheque
for £200 to cover her travel expenses to Surrey; to pay the staff
wages; and to keep the household running. It was two weeks
before Fred and Emmeline were bailed. Meanwhile, the police
searched Mary's flat looking for Christabel Pankhurst.

The trial of the WSPU leaders in May 1912 provided a
huge amount of publicity for the women's cause. Under
Evelyn Sharp's editorship, *Votes for Women* devoted densely
packed pages in every edition regarding the trial: the

prosecution and defence arguments and the summing up, and presented portraits of the imprisoned leaders. Crowds thronged the streets outside the Old Bailey hoping to catch a glimpse of the celebrity suffragettes. The press reported the cross-examinations and detailed what the women wore and the flowers they carried. The charges against Mabel Tuke were dropped but Mrs Pankhurst, Fred and Emmeline were convicted and sentenced to nine months. Fred and Mrs Pankhurst were also ordered to pay the costs of the trial.

Mary and May Start jointly kept the households in London and Surrey running during Emmeline and Fred's imprisonment. Mary visited Emmeline to discuss Esperance business. May Start also requested to be allowed to visit, writing to the prison governor that her employer had three properties to run (the London and Surrey homes and the Sundial hostel), to which he replied that people with three properties to run should take care not to find themselves in prison. Emmeline and Mrs Pankhurst were placed in adjoining cells; both immediately went on hunger strike. Knowing that Emmeline would be forcibly fed, Mary feared that she would be unable to eat when she was invited to dinner by the Shakespearean scholar Israel Gollancz to discuss her dancers' participation in an event at Earls Court that summer.

Following her forcible feeding, Emmeline was released; Fred, also on hunger strike, was released a few weeks later. After recuperating from their ordeal in Surrey, the couple set off for Switzerland. On their way they stopped in Boulogne to discuss plans for the coming autumn campaign with Mrs Pankhurst and Christabel. A disagreement ensued as to the wisdom of stepping up the campaign of property damage to include arson. Emmeline and Fred feared that if they did so the movement would lose the goodwill of the public and harden opposition. They did not regard the disagreement as serious, however, and travelled on to Switzerland and then to visit Emmeline's brother in Canada. In New York they received a letter from Mrs Pankhurst warning them that she feared the government now saw Fred's wealth as a means of attacking the WSPU and urging them to remove their assets to Canada where they should remain and lead the movement there. As long as he and Emmeline remained in leadership positions, she warned, repeated conspiracy trials would see him targeted, with costs of thousands of pounds ordered against him and business owners repeatedly pursuing him for damages. The knowledge that this was the likely consequence of their actions was likely to deter women from mounting attacks against property. And if the organisation were to reimburse Fred for his losses, its funds would be diverted via Fred, into government coffers. He would become a weapon with which to damage the organisation and reduce its effectiveness; he also risked personal ruin. Despite this warning, the couple announced their intention of returning to the struggle that autumn, no matter what the risk to their own wealth.

On 13 August 1912, while the Pethick-Lawrences were in Canada and Mary and May Start were still responsible for overseeing Emmeline's affairs, a conference was held in Stratford to discuss the differences in approach between Sharp and Mary. It should, Mary contended, have been held before the decision the previous year to award the position of director of the dance school to Sharp. Familiar arguments were trotted out by supporters of each. On Mary's side the militant-supporting Lady Isabel Margesson told the audience that 'before children acquired accuracy they needed power'. It was a phrase adopted by the composer and folk song collector Ralph Vaughan Williams when he attended a fancy-dress party as a caricature Mary with a placard hung about his neck reading 'Power before Accuracy'. On Sharp's side, Archibald Flower stressed the need for accuracy in teaching. Reviewers and reporters took their own stance: the *School of Music Review* supported Sharp's position, telling readers that 'the aim must be to achieve faultless accuracy'. J. Kenneth Curwen in the *Musical Herald* countered that education should be a 'pleasure not a labour' and that there need be no fear of 'over insistence on the correct traditional ritual'. These positions were predictable since the *School of Music Review* was published by Novello which also published Sharp, and Curwen published the Esperance works. Both combatants tended to exaggerate their differences, with Sharp characterising Mary for being all about fun and no technique, and Mary accusing Sharp of being formal, pedantic and joyless. In reality, there was not such a great split in what they were presenting. *The Times* writer was bemused at what appeared in practical terms to be a spat over nothing: 'The spirit of joy which has been the chief characteristic of the one and the spirit of accuracy which has marked the other are now to be found in the classes of the teachers. To the onlooker their aims and methods seem to have become practically identical.'

Mary's dancers would not appear at the Stratford school, instead they spent the summer performing for crowds of visitors at the 'Shakespeare's England' exhibition at Earl's Court. Organised by Winston Churchill's mother, the exhibition lasted sixteen weeks and presented visitors with a town of replica buildings – houses, almshouses, market halls, and even a full replica of Shakespeare's Globe Theatre designed by Edwin Lutyens. Visitors experienced costumed events, jousting, theatrical performances, historical recreations and Morris dancing. Mary formed a team of the best young people she had trained from all over the country to perform a daily song and dance programme. The exhibition attracted huge crowds. King George V and Queen Mary visited with the prime minister for a special performance in July where Mary wore Elizabethan dress. It was a source of great pride to the Esperance dancers to have danced for the king. Following the Esperance's successful residency, Mary was commissioned to write a book on the English folk revival with Frank Kidson. It would be her opportunity to claim the Esperance's place in Morris history.

The Pethick-Lawrences arrived back in England on the 2 October to the news (probably delivered by May Start) that Mrs Pankhurst had moved the WSPU's offices to new premises and set aside no space for them there. On arriving at the new offices in Holborn, they were met with embarrassed silence from Mabel Tuke and Annie Kenney. Mrs Pankhurst informed them that their involvement with the WSPU was at an end. Members would be informed at the forthcoming rally at the Albert Hall that they had been unable to approve the forthcoming campaign of arson and that they and the Pankhursts had therefore agreed to go their separate ways. A shocked Emmeline insisted that an emergency meeting of the committee be convened, which Mary attended with Elizabeth Robins. Neither the Pankhursts nor Mabel Tuke would shake Emmeline or Fred's hands. Mrs Pankhurst announced that where confidence no longer existed working together was impossible. Fred was reminded that he was not a member of the organisation and not allowed to speak. When Mary and Elizabeth Robins attempted to protest they were told that they had rarely attended meetings and ought to have better informed themselves of the facts. Emmeline and Fred walked out. Annie Kenney decided to remain with the Pankhursts, but, she said, 'the old days were over. That was quite clear to me ... Christabel won, the fight continued, but the Movement, as a Movement, lost. The two had gone who had been the creative geniuses of the constructive side of a world-famed fight.' Mary left the WSPU and its committee on the spot, as did Elizabeth Robins.

'There was no appeal against our expulsion from the WSPU,' wrote Fred. 'Mrs Pankhurst was the acknowledged autocrat of the Union.' What hurt them most was not the decision; Fred at least appreciated the practical reasons for it: Mrs Pankhurst could now run the organisation as she saw fit, without having to take into account the opinions of her treasurer or to worry about the impact of Fred's wealth being targeted. Nor, other than Christabel, was there anyone remaining in the organisation with the public profile to represent a threat to her authority. It was the underhand manner with which the expulsion was engineered that hurt. Mrs Pankhurst had moved the organisation's offices without informing her closest comrades who had stood trial and endured prison with her, and she had a substitute magazine already in production to replace *Votes for Women* before she had even spoken to them. 'The whole situation has come upon us with startling suddenness and at the same time nearly stunned us,' wrote Fred to his friend the Labour MP George Lansbury. 'To be asked to leave the WSPU to which we had contributed our life blood was like asking a mother to be parted from her child.'

The Pethick-Lawrences considered appealing to the members to back them on the proposed policy of escalating property damage. But the members had never debated policy in a democratic manner and Emmeline and Fred had no desire to split the ranks. They agreed to say nothing in the hope of reducing damage to the organisation. 'We refused to pull down,' wrote Fred, 'stone by stone, the edifice which we had, with such care and at such cost, assisted to build up.' The Pethick-Lawrences took *Votes for Women* with them and ran it as an independent suffrage magazine. The WSPU launched *The Suffragette* in its place. For a while, Evelyn Sharp trod a careful line, remaining a member of the WSPU but editing an independent journal. In November 1912, Emmeline and Fred set up the Votes for Women Fellowship, attracting a loose group of suffragists who, for one reason or another, were not part of the WSPU: men; family and close associates like Mary and Alfred Sayer, the WSPU's auditor; those who had always been opposed to militancy; those who had become uncomfortable at the escalation in property damage; and those who could not separate the women's campaign from socialism in general. The Pethick-Lawrences now provided a base around which left-leaning suffragists, moderate militants and social reformers coalesced.

Mrs Pankhurst's fears about government targeting the Pethick-Lawrences' wealth proved correct. The Director of Public Prosecutions took action against Fred for recovery of the costs of the conspiracy trial. (Mrs Pankhurst had no assets and was not worth pursuing.) He refused to pay on the grounds that he had risked his life and health in support of the cause and was not going to back down over money. The bailiffs were put into the couple's country home and their household goods auctioned. Claims for compensation followed from numerous business owners whose windows had been smashed. Fred was temporarily bankrupted so that monies could be recovered from his accounts.

While Emmeline and Mary were embroiled in the fallout from the split, Cecil Sharp was consolidating his position as the leader of the folk revival. He had now published numerous books of instruction and was supplying trained teachers all over the country. He had set up a men's side and when the theatre director Harley Granville Barker suggested approaching Mary to provide dancers for a production of *A Winter's Tale* he denounced her side's 'hoydenish gambols' and offered his own services instead. In December 1912, he promoted his English Folk Dance Society with a show at London's Savoy theatre. In a letter to Flower, he admitted himself satisfied with the reviews, noting with pleasure the absence of sentimentality and any 'Merrie England business'. But within days Mary and the Esperance were also dancing to a large London audience, once more at the Queen's Hall. Characteristically, *Votes for Women* carried a long piece about the Esperance Guild of Morris Dancers who had 'danced into the hearts of the public'. Like Sharp, Mary was pleased at her dancers' reception, reporting that the hall was full and that the enthusiasm of the audience as keen as ever. 'In their quaint costumes one is transported to bygone days,' she reported, 'when dancing was an important part of English national life ... when English lads and lasses had their own dances and songs, and took a healthy joy in the invigorating pastime.' In comparison to the quick brain and nimble feet needed for the Morris, she found the polka and waltz decadent and verging on degeneracy.

At Christmas, Mary wrote that the past year had been the best she had ever had, despite the ongoing feud. But, perhaps anticipating that her position would be further undermined, she told Clive Carey that she gave thanks that she was neither financially nor intellectually reliant on the movement.

> If it does not want my work anymore on the same lines, there is plenty else to do. But even the troubles have brought me some very staunch friends and some very dear people into my life, that is worth a lot, so we won't worry about it any more, but go head the best way we can.

Reflecting on the situation in the *Bystander* at the close of the year, Francis Toye, the music critic of *Vanity Fair* who had collected dances with Mary, mused irreverently that jealousies and quarrels seemed to be inseparable from the name of Morris, and were so vicious that practitioners would soon have to be registered as members of a dangerous trade, so exposed were its exponents to attack from within the movement. He summed the situation thus:

> If you join the Esperance Club you are excommunicated by the Folk Dance Society; if you are a member of the latter you are anathema to the former. And so it goes on, as those interested know, throughout the length and breadth of England. The only things that suffers is the common cause of the Morris Dancing and those of us who are more for the spirit than the letter are left to answer the scoffers at the whole movement as best we may. It would be quite amusing, had we not grown thoroughly disgusted with the whole subject.

Chapter Seven

Exile, War and the Vote 1913–1918

By the end of 1912, Emmeline had been ousted from the national committee of the WSPU and Cecil Sharp had wrested leadership of the dance revival from Mary. Emmeline never really forgave Mrs Pankhurst for the manner of her dismissal from the organisation to which she had given six years of her life. Mary's sense of betrayal by Sharp was never concealed. But neither was driven primarily by personal ambition and both remained undaunted in their commitment to the pursuit of social change.

Mary continued to lead the Esperance dancers as they travelled the country. An entertaining raconteur, she used her experiences when out collecting dances with Clive Carey to provide colour for her talks and interviews. She recalled one old man playing tunes for her propped up in his bed, another fiddling as they travelled, with Carey dutifully noting down the tunes. The dancers remained in demand and the press no less interested in their activities than in the feud with Sharp. In May 1913, Lady Betty Balfour, sister of Lady Constance Lytton, engaged Blanche Payling to instruct schoolteachers in Woking, where she was president of the Conservative and Unionist Women's Franchise Association. Over 200 newly taught children then danced in the Empire Day celebrations there. Shortly afterwards, the dancers performed at London's

Globe Theatre with the traditional Bampton side, giving Mary an opportunity to refute Cecil Sharp's claims of inaccuracy once again. She explained to the press that watching the Bampton side and the Esperance team side-by-side, the audience could see that there was little difference between the traditional dancers and those they had taught. The difference between her dancers and Sharp's was one of social class; 'the average young lady or gentleman' could not get near the spirit of the dance, she said, but her company could as they were 'working lads and lasses from town and country'. To put it in terms we would recognise today, Sharp's sides, she implied, were appropriating working-class culture and gentrifying it.

Loyalties often came down to personal relationships and political sympathies; press coverage in papers with whom Mary shared a political vision tended to be sympathetic to her arguments against Sharp and his English Folk Dance Society. Her friends at *Votes for Women* described the dancing of her young men as 'especially worth of praise in its vigour and zest, combined with gracefulness'. The *Westminster Gazette* reported that 'with the Esperance dancers it is more than a dance; it is the expression and embodiment of a very real gaiety, a vivid exhilaration'.

Notwithstanding their ejection from the WSPU, Mary and Emmeline continued to campaign for the vote. In July, Mary spoke alongside Fred Pethick-Lawrence at a meeting of the Votes for Women Fellowship at the Portman Rooms. She reminded the assembled company of why they were fighting for political influence for women, once again drawing on personal experience of working with those whose lives were lived 'in the raw' and held 'cheap'. Her speech formed the basis of another long piece in *Votes for Women* – now edited jointly by Fred and Evelyn Sharp – entitled 'People who Matter and some who don't'. In August 1913, Evelyn was in prison with Emmeline and Lady Sybil Smith after protesting at the use of the Prisoners (Temporary Discharge for Ill-health) Act 1913. The Act allowed women on hunger strike to be released from prison when dangerously ill and to be brought back into prison as soon as they were sufficiently recovered to complete their sentences. The strategy undermined the hunger strike and ensured that women served their full sentences but repeated starvations had a detrimental effect on the health of the women concerned. It was dubbed the 'Cat and Mouse Act' by Fred in *Votes for Women*, a term which stuck in the public imagination. Emmeline led a group of protestors from various women's suffrage societies down Whitehall to the Houses of Parliament. Evelyn Sharp joined her as representative of the Women Writers' Suffrage League. On trying to make a speech in the lobby of the House of Commons, Emmeline was arrested. Bailed overnight, she addressed a meeting that evening at Kingsway Hall, where she claimed that she had been flung down steps and arrested for going to the aid of Lady Sybil. All three were sentenced to fourteen days. On her release from Holloway, Evelyn's brother invited her to join him in Stratford. She declined but they agreed not to quarrel on the suffrage issue – though she told him that she was not convinced that he was totally opposed. She also urged Cecil and Mary to put aside their feud. She later said that she believed that the root of their dispute was not the dance, but women's suffrage, and that without Mary's involvement in the fight for the vote, and her involvement of the dancers in it, all other issues could have been settled between them.

Despite Mary's continuing efforts to maintain the profile and reputation of the Esperance Guild, the momentum in the Morris revival was now with Evelyn's brother. Sharp's teaching capacity had outgrown that of the Esperance. More than 450 people participated in dance training in Stratford in 1913 and the newly trained teachers could be expected to hold classes all over the nation. Sharp was also publishing prolifically and branches of the English Folk Dance Society were being set up across the country. Outside the structures of the Stratford programme and with no national society to support her, Mary's Esperance Guild could not compete. People who had supported her vision began to drift towards what now looked to be the future of the movement.

Unlike Sharp, who had dedicated his life to the folk revival, Mary was seemingly unable (or unwilling) to turn down calls for assistance in other causes. In September, she travelled to Ireland to speak on the dance revival at a gathering of musicians and academics from across Europe at the Giant's Causeway. She was accompanied by Blanche Payling, who taught the delegates to dance. At the end of the week, she took a train to Dublin at Emmeline's request. A prolonged strike at the Jacob's biscuit factory was causing hardship amongst unpaid factory workers and Emmeline sent Mary as an envoy to offer relief to strikers' hungry children. If Mary could persuade the strike leaders to allow a party of children to cross to England, Emmeline proposed to house them in the holiday cottage that she had built for Esperance holidays. But Catholic community leaders were reluctant to allow the children to leave for a Protestant foster home. Mary contacted a priest at the Brompton Oratory, who had an interest in the Morris, to obtain a letter of introduction and assurance that arrangements would be made for the children to hear Mass and telegraphed Emmeline to ask if she might bring one of the mothers to supervise the children and ensure that no attempts were made to proselytise. Emmeline arranged access to the Roman Catholic chapel of her neighbour, the Anglo-Irish peer Lord Ashbourne, to enable the children to hear Mass. With religious leaders suitably reassured, permission to travel was granted and Mary escorted the Irish children by boat and train to Surrey. On arrival they were found to be so lice-ridden that a farm labourer-come-barber sheared off their hair and burnt it. When Emmeline went to speak about women's suffrage in Dublin the following year, she found the children waiting for her, dressed in the green jerseys that her sister had given them in Holmwood.

After Mary and Emmeline's departure from the WSPU, attacks on property escalated. With the introduction of the 'Cat and Mouse' Act, the hunger strike had lost its efficacy; window-smashing was now accompanied by damage to golf links, stadiums and churches and arson attacks on letter boxes and private residences. This provoked hostility and entrenched the government's position. It also dismayed moderate campaigners. In the absence of Emmeline and Fred's day-to-day supervision, the WSPU's organisation had grown chaotic, with Christabel leading from Paris and many of the other remaining leaders in and out of prison. The authorities targeted the organisation's funders, suppliers and supporters, driving its operations underground. Donations dropped, finances were in disarray and the infrastructure of the organisation disintegrated with headquarters forced to move from house to house. As actions became more sporadic and more personal in nature, many ordinary members who had been dismayed at Emmeline and Fred's departure the previous year, and had never really understood the reasons behind it, petitioned Mrs Pankhurst for their return.

Henry Nevinson, observing the strained relationship between WSPU headquarters and its supporters, concluded that the organisation's strength was slipping away. He proposed the formation of a new, moderately militant organisation in February 1914. The United Suffragists would be open to men and women and – unlike the WSPU – it would have a democratic constitution. Evelyn Sharp joined its first committee alongside Nevinson and a number of disaffected high-profile WSPU supporters. Laurence Housman, who had first suggested that the Esperance dancers give public performances, became one of the association's vice-presidents. Mary joined Evelyn and Nevinson in the new organisation and a few months later Fred and Emmeline dissolved the Votes for Women Fellowship and gave *Votes for Women* to the United Suffragists as its house journal. Evelyn would continue as the journal's editor while Emmeline accepted a place on the organisation's committee and planned a suffrage tour of the world, to start in the United States that September. The new grouping adopted purple as one of its colours, alongside gold and white, and the motto *Usque ad finem*: 'until the end'.

In the early months of 1914, Mary took up a campaign for the release of a desperate widow convicted of neglecting her children. Sarah Savage had been sentenced to six months' hard labour for child cruelty when it was discovered that she had kept three children secretly locked away in squalor at her lodgings while she went out to work. It was Emmeline who alerted Mary to the case. Both suspected a miscarriage of justice. Mary interviewed everyone involved and ascertained that Mrs Savage had not hidden her children due to laziness or neglect but because she had no money for shoes and could not send them to school. She had been terrified that if the authorities discovered that she was unable to feed her family they would be taken from her and placed in the workhouse or fostered out; given the choice between living a pitifully degraded existence or having her family broken up, she had chosen to keep them together in secrecy. For Mary and Emmeline this highlighted the way in which the law worked against women in desperate circumstances, forcing them to make impossible choices. Such, they believed, would be reviewed if women had the vote. Using contacts, she managed to gain a meeting with an under-secretary at the Home Office (only after making it quite clear that the appointment was not about a suffrage matter or she would not have been admitted). She was granted permission to meet Mrs Savage in prison. She reported that she had found a 'frail old woman with a pathetic smile and a crushed manner'. Illiterate and barely educated, Sarah Savage was the living embodiment of the inequality that Mary and Emmeline had been fighting all their lives. Mary reported Mrs Savage's plight in *Votes for Women* and was quoted in the House of Lords when questions were raised about the case. In early March, the Home Office agreed to release Mrs Savage from Holloway into Mary's care, despite her being a known suffragette. Mary took the woman to her own home, found her lodgings and arranged for her to visit her children in the workhouse. Readers of *Votes for Women* raised funds for furniture and clothes.

Unlike the now-professional folklorist Cecil Sharp, Mary was juggling her involvement in the dance revival with such welfare interventions, campaigning journalism and her involvement with the United Suffragists. In the summer of 1914, the dance revival took her to Bristol where the dancers were performing at the International Exhibition. Her exhibition team of working people comprised a brass foundry worker, a book finisher, a leather worker, a shoemaker, a gilder, an embroiderer, a paper pattern-maker and a seamstress. As ever, Mary took the opportunity to set out her vision to the local press. A long piece in the *Somerset Gazette*, which credited her with having saved the Morris from oblivion, reported Mary describing the revival as her 'special hobby' and herself as an enthusiast with many irons in the fire. This was surely a pointed barb at Sharp's wish to professionalise the movement. The Morris, she said, was amateur, the dance of the working classes who could dance it accurately, without any thought of what the 'cultured' called 'technique'.

Mary told the paper that her aim was to rejuvenate England through the Morris. Her presence in Bristol was not simply to oversee the dancers, however; she had become the honorary secretary of a proposed Arthurian festival to be held in Glastonbury that August. The project's founder was the socialist composer Rutland Boughton. He planned to establish a new national theatre in the town and to stage an annual festival of music, drama and dance inspired by Wagner's Bayreuth. The new national summer festival would draw on Glastonbury's connection with Arthurian myths. Like Mary, Boughton believed in the power of music to encourage new thinking and to transform lives. Festival productions would be staged by local people in collaboration with professional musicians. The scheme was supported by such high-profile musicians as Sir Thomas Beecham, Gustav Holst and the writer George Bernard Shaw and the foundation stone for the new theatre was to have been laid by Sir Edward Elgar. Boughton's socialist politics and ambition to use music to promote social change would have struck an obvious chord with Mary. But did she also have hopes that this West Country national theatre, with its annual festival, might have folk elements to rival those of Stratford? Boughton was certainly familiar with the folk movement; his librettist, Reginald Buckley, had been involved in the Stratford festival and worked with Mary to publish a history of the Stratford movement. In all likelihood, it was Buckley who had recommended Mary to Boughton. Did Mary also hope that if she was involved from the beginning, she might establish a teaching base in the west of England to rival Sharp's in the Midlands? It seems quite likely, but circumstances were against her.

Europe was moving inexorably towards war even as Mary spoke to the Somerset press. The heir to the Austrian empire, Archduke Franz Ferdinand, had been assassinated in Sarajevo at the end of June 1914. Plans for the Arthurian festival at Glastonbury, due to open just as war was declared on August 4, were scaled back. Mrs Pankhurst and Christabel announced that the WSPU would abandon the struggle for the vote, to the astonished outrage of many of their supporters. Victory, they said, must take precedence over women's enfranchisement. In the face of possible invasion as German troops marched across France, they had little choice but to abandon the militant campaign if they were not to be accused of undermining their nation in a time of war. But the decision, taken without consultation of members, dismayed many of their followers. Other campaigning societies also announced the suspension of all 'political' work and urged members to devote their energies to the relief of distress occasioned by the war.

For Emmeline, the cause of international peace was a natural extension of her fight for women's rights; to her, the outbreak of war was confirmation of the folly of leaving political power solely in the hands of men. For many other radical campaigners, the war confirmed their commitment to fighting for women's involvement in the political process. In contrast to the other national women's suffrage organisations, the United Suffragists announced that it would continue to campaign as a single-issue organisation and late 1914 saw an influx of disappointed WSPU members, pacifists and others who questioned the necessity of war. Evelyn Sharp took more practical action, refusing to pay her taxes throughout the war on the grounds that she had no vote on whether her taxes were used to wage a war that she did not support, and therefore she ought not to have any liability to pay tax to fund it. Under her editorship, *Votes for Women* continued to address issues of social justice and inequality as women's experience of low wages, exploitation, financial insecurity, bad housing and child mortality were now exacerbated by the uncertainties and disruptions of war. The paper exposed the exploitation of women undertaking war work being paid less than men for doing the same jobs, and the hypocrisy of those who had told women that their place was in the home now urging women out into paid work with few of the protections or the benefits afforded to men. The United Suffragists also took practical action, setting up a women's club in Southwark with the aim of alleviating some of the suffering exacerbated by the war. It was run by Mary Phillips, a WSPU paid organiser who had been the campaign's longest-serving prisoner. On being sacked by Christabel Pankhurst, she had gone to work with Sylvia Pankhurst's East End Federation of the Suffragettes in Canning Town. Performances by Mary's dancers raised funds to cover the club's operating costs.

Shortly after the outbreak of war, Emmeline travelled to the United States to inaugurate a new suffrage campaign there. She saw this as an opportunity to enlist the support of the suffrage movement in neutral America in the cause of a negotiated peace in Europe. Travelling with the National Women's Peace Party on a tour billed the 'Women's War on

War', she resigned her position with the United Suffragists in order to be able to speak freely to American audiences. Back in London, Evelyn Sharp regularly reported on her progress. Evelyn's brother also left Britain for the United States. With most cultural activities suspended lest they deter men from enlisting or distract women from using their leisure time in support of the war effort, there was little prospect of him making a living in England. He had arranged the folk music and dances for Harley Granville Barker's controversial West End production of *A Midsummer Night's Dream* at the Savoy Theatre; now he was invited to the United States to assist with the New York production. He sailed in hope of finding lecturing and other work there. Two years later, he and Maud Karpeles travelled to the Appalachian Mountains to collect English folk songs, which they later published in *English Folk Songs from the Southern Appalachians*.

After nearly twenty years, Mary closed the Esperance Club and the activities of the Esperance Guild ceased as her team scattered. Geoffrey Toye, with whom she had worked on the second Esperance Morris book, joined up, as did many of her male dancers, and her girls were called into munitions and other war work. With such demands on their time there was little scope for club work. Mary continued to combine her commitment to alleviating the suffering of the poor, achieving the vote for women, and promoting the Morris dance as best she could with the few performers available. Often the three aims coalesced. In March 1915, the Esperance dancers gave a performance in Islington as part of an initiative to lift the spirits of women whose fathers and husbands were at the front; the following week Mary led them in a performance to raise funds for the United Suffragists' women's club in Southwark with Evelyn Sharp at her side to speak about the work of the club. In May, she spoke on behalf of the United Suffragists at a meeting organised by the Church League for Women's Suffrage to call for women's interests to be protected during and after the war. Alongside her on the platform was Mary Richardson, the woman who had achieved notoriety before the outbreak of war when she slashed the *Rokeby Venus* in the National Gallery. The following month, Mary took the Esperance dancers to Surbiton where she spoke at a gathering of local teachers. But the impact of the war overshadowed everything. The days of the Esperance travelling the country were over; their engagements now were generally within the greater London area and focused on addressing women's issues.

In the spring of 1915, Emmeline returned to Europe with the American delegation to attend the International Women's Congress for Peace in the Hague. She was one of only three British delegates to reach the conference as the British government closed ferry routes and refused delegates permission to travel. Evelyn Sharp was one of those refused a passport. The Women's International League (now the Women's International League for Peace and Freedom) was founded at that Congress and Emmeline became treasurer of the British branch. She spent the rest of the war campaigning for peace and women's suffrage in print and at public meetings. As the war progressed, more and more ex-suffragettes joined her in the Women's International League and the United Suffragists. Had women like Mary, Emmeline, Evelyn Sharp and their associates not kept the issue of the vote for women in the minds of politicians during the war years the cause might have slipped from the political agenda. They ensured that this did not happen, despite accusations that to carry on campaigning was unpatriotic and a distraction from the war effort.

English Folk Song and Dance, written the previous year by Mary Neal and Frank Kidson, was published in 1915 in circumstances that could not have been foreseen when it was written. Arriving in a country preoccupied with war, it did not have the impact that Mary had surely hoped for. Once again, Mary stressed her claim to have been at the forefront of the Morris revival. Before 1905, she told readers, few people even knew that England had folk dances, and fewer still practised them, and only then at festivals in country villages. She speculated on the origins of the dance. As she had suggested in her introduction to the second Esperance Morris book, she now believed that some of the dances had their origins in the expression of primitive beliefs and magical ceremonial. Quoting Frazer's 'Golden Bough', she allied English folk dance with the sun worship and ceremonial of ancient cultures, seeing echoes of supposed sacrifice and magic in the moves and steps. Though she revelled in the possibility that the dances might date back to pre-Christian times, she admitted that all religious significance had disappeared and that the dance now represented the English peasant in holiday mood; a combination of boisterous revelry and sport.

She had dedicated herself to presenting the joy of these 'peasant' revelries and protecting them from the obsessive experts who would change them. Now she confessed herself unhappy with the 'garb' adopted by dancers which did just that. Dress, she claimed, had 'fallen into evil ways'. In terms as prescriptive of any of Sharp's, she set out the correct attire, based upon those customarily worn by the Headington Quarrymen when she had first seen them: a white shirt and white flannel or dark trousers for men; for girls, a sun bonnet or hat decorated with ribbons or flowers, a simple cotton frock, and ribbons at the waist. If attire must be fancy dress, she wrote, it should be Elizabethan. Most importantly of all, 'ordinary' shoes should be worn and not dancing shoes. For the Morris was the dance of the countryside, the peasantry and the field and not of the ballroom or dancing studio: 'any sort of thin ballet shoe is quite out of place and spoils the character of the open air dance'. The *Musical Times* reviewer, presumably on Sharp's side of the divide, dismissed Mary's section on the dance as 'an object lesson in uncritical method [that] is difficult to take seriously'. Such esoteric arguments were surely perceived by readers as being rather irrelevant now that regular cultural performances had fallen victim to the needs of the war. Indeed, of Sharp's male side, four young men, including the composer George Butterworth, were to be killed on the Somme the following year.

The year 1916 also saw the death of Mary's original collaborator in the dance revival. For several years, Herbert McIlwaine had worked alongside her as musical director of the Esperance; he had introduced her to folk music and to Cecil Sharp. He and Mary had ceased working together as he could not agree with her support for the militant suffrage movement. But despite the fact that McIlwaine had gone on to accompany Sharp to Oxfordshire to collect dances for the third Morris book, he and Mary had remained on good terms. His death, at the age of 57, was a blow to her. He left a young widow and a toddler son.

Mary was now living and working in the Poplar area of East London. On the closure of the Esperance Club, the warden of Toynbee Hall had asked her to join the project on its wartime relocation from Whitechapel to London's docklands. She had left the flat that she had shared with Emmeline and was now living in a house on the river. Though residing in a deprived neighbourhood, she was happy in what she described as the only 'good' house in the street:

> It had panelled rooms, beautiful mantelpieces and a quite wonderful staircase. At the back, there was a little paved garden with a flower bed in the middle, a vine on one side and a very large fig tree on the other. But the great attraction was the river, which at high tide flowed right up to the garden wall. All the shipping of the world went by and from a wooden balcony at the back I could have spoken to those on board.

She let the top- and ground-floor flats and lived in the rest of the house.

With conscription applying to all able-bodied men of military age from early 1916, women were being drafted to fill positions in vital services. Mary took up work in pensions administration for dock workers. It was a means of contributing to the welfare of working people. She found the population of Poplar quite different to that of the West End where the Esperance Club had operated. The population around St Pancras worked in the richest area of London, as servants in the grand houses or in trades that serviced them; they were used to kowtowing to their social betters. The men of Poplar were dockers, stevedores and boiler men, working at the hundreds of docks that brought goods in from across the world to the capital of the empire. Mary found the men a very different breed, more confident and demanding of their pension rights than the humbler, even 'cringing', working men that she had been used to assisting. But though they knew their rights and demanded them, Mary still felt that their legal dues were not what they ought morally to have been entitled to. And while the men were away at war, she fought for the rights of their dependents.

Conditions for the volunteers were grim. Mary was working without salary or expenses, paying for her own food and fares. And when the office moved from the Toynbee Hall outpost in Poplar to a room above a fish and chip shop, there was no carpeting and no more furniture than a basic desk and chair. It was a far remove from her comfortable upbringing in Birmingham with servants and carriages. But she was doing what she had always done, fighting for the fair treatment of working people, and particularly for women and children. When the widows of the 'missing' (who had no death certificate as their bodies had not been recovered and identified), were denied payouts by insurance companies she took their case to the Pensions Office in Whitehall.

By 1917, the German naval blockade of shipping had led to severe food shortages and Londoners' nights were disturbed by air attacks that caused terror and panic. On the early evening of 19 January 1917, Mary was in her sitting room in the Isle of Dogs when the front bay windows of her home were blown in. The cause, a huge explosion at the Silvertown munitions works in West Ham, killed 73 people and injured 400. The factory was destroyed, as were many nearby buildings, and debris was spread for miles around. Up to 70,000 properties were damaged, with nearly 1,000 destroyed or irreparably damaged. The blast was heard over 100 miles away and thousands were made homeless. Already exhausted from lack of sleep, Mary suffered severe shock. She attributed the explosion with bringing on an attack of neuritis, a debilitating inflammation of the nervous system. It is not clear what the cause of Mary's nervous condition was, as neuritis can have bacterial or autoimmune causes, but exhaustion, hunger, stress and shock were no doubt contributory factors. She was taken to Glasgow to recover with a female doctor friend.

Mary's illness probably explains her low profile in the last months of the campaign for the vote for women. Emmeline and Evelyn Sharp had repeatedly warned readers of *Votes for Women* of the danger of dropping the campaign during the war years on the basis of vague promises of reform after the war was won. By 1917, many who had abandoned the campaign in the early days of the war had returned to it, disappointed that the politicians who had advised them to cease campaigning on the outbreak of war now claimed that there was no longer any evidence that women still wanted the vote. The United

Suffragists' membership now comprised a broad spectrum of ex-WSPU activists and non-militant NUWSS supporters who were ready to push the women's cause when Lloyd George's government proposed a bill to give the vote to all men over 21. That the organisation still existed was largely down to the efforts of Evelyn Sharp; whereas Emmeline and Christabel Pankhurst's energies had been diverted into the war effort, and Emmeline Pethick-Lawrence's to opposing it, Evelyn Sharp had continued to promote the cause throughout the war, editing *Votes for Women* as a women's war paper throughout. She was declared bankrupt in 1917 for non-payment of taxes and lost her books and her typewriter when her possessions were confiscated by the tax authorities. As writing was her only income, this was a great hardship. Mary and Emmeline were amongst those who clubbed together to replace her furniture.

It was the United Suffragists, led by Evelyn Sharp, who proposed the Speaker's Conference of 1916 out of which came the 1918 reform bill. The government's aim was to ensure that all those who had fought were entitled to vote; many serving men were under voting age, did not meet the property requirements or had been away so long that they no longer met residency requirements. But the prime minister was open to appeals that the vote might also be given to a limited number of women. Women's war work is often credited with having achieved in a few years what generations of peaceful campaigning and a decade of militancy had not. But it is unlikely that the vote would have been granted to women were it not for those who kept the issue on the political agenda throughout the war years, and to the threat of a return to militancy once the war was over. It was Evelyn Sharp's opinion that ministers' claims that women had done their bit and thereby proved their worth during the war were no more than a face-saver that allowed them to grant the vote to a limited number of women without having to admit that they had capitulated to the argument of militancy. The Representation of the People Act 1918 enfranchised over 8.5 million women over the age of 30 who were either qualified as householders to vote in local elections, were married to householders, or who occupied property worth over £5 in value, or who were graduates. Men were entitled to vote from 21. The fact that women were not granted the vote on the same terms as men ensured that men remained the electoral majority. Far from rewarding the primarily younger women who had worked in the factories and on the land, it was older, middle-class women who met the criteria. At the United Suffragists' victory celebration at Caxton Hall in 1918, Evelyn Sharp was presented with a book containing the signatures of many members in gratitude at her having brought *Votes for Women* through the war.

The war years had taken a toll on those who had initiated the dance revival; Herbert McIlwaine was dead; Cecil Sharp's wife had suffered a heart attack and his son was wounded at the front; Lady Constance Lytton had suffered a series of strokes (blamed by her family on the effects of forcible feeding) and was now an invalid; Emmeline and Fred Pethick-Lawrence had been forced to leave the flat that had been the WSPU's first London office after it suffered war damage and was requisitioned by the Air Ministry; and Mary Neal was struggling with post-traumatic shock and a debilitating nervous illness after Silvertown. Now in her late fifties, tired and worn down by deprivations of war, Mary decided to leave the city that had been her life and her home for thirty years.

Henry Nevinson (1856–1941)

Evelyn Sharp's partner for many years was the campaigning journalist and war correspondent, Henry Woodd Nevinson. The son of a solicitor, he came to radical politics in a similar manner to Emmeline and Mary, after teaching the poor in London's East End. Nevinson's wife, Margaret Wynne Nevinson née Jones, was a member of the WSPU and Nevinson was a close friend of Fred Pethick-Lawrence.

As a war correspondent he reported from Turkey, South Africa, Russia, India the Balkans and the Middle East. Women's suffrage was just one of the radical causes which he supported. He also organised relief work in Macedonia and Albania, worked for the Friends' Ambulance Service during the First World War, and campaigned against bonded servitude in the Angolan cocoa plantations.

After being estranged from his wife, Nevinson had a long-term relationship – due to social mores of the day, not publicly acknowledged – with Evelyn Sharp from 1901. He attended his first WSPU meeting with her in 1907 and was a founder member of the Men's League for Women's Suffrage (MLWS). He admired the courage and determination of the militants, and with other prominent male supporters such as Fred Pethick-Lawrence and George Lansbury he worked to allay fears that the women's movement was a war against men. He continued to speak for the WSPU and to march with it, even after his wife left to form the Women's Freedom League in 1907, and resigned his post at *The Daily News* in protest at the paper's refusal to condemn forcible feeding. He considered the MLWS insufficiently radical and went on to found the militant Men's Political Union for Women's Enfranchisement. Nevinson regarded the split between the Pankhursts and the Pethick-Lawrences as highly detrimental and was a founder member of the United Suffragists. After the war, he and Evelyn were joined by Mary and Emmeline in the Kibbo Kift youth movement.

Chapter Eight

'A Masculine Rhythm': 1919 to the Present Day

At the end of the war, Mary left London and moved to Sussex, where she and Emmeline had spent so many happy summers with the Esperance girls. She made her home in the village of Amberley. She was planning a period of complete rest, but though the Esperance had fallen victim to the war, the Morris remained part of her political vision, and she continued to promote its benefits alongside her campaigning activities. In September 1919, she was back in Oxford, at an event hosted by the Women's International League for Peace and Freedom. In response to the physical, cultural and emotional devastation of modern warfare, she looked to the music of the past to bring harmony and strength to a shattered society, as she had looked to 'Merrie England' to heal the ills of pre-war spiritual deprivation. Folk music, she told her audience, was good for the development of personality, healing and strengthening. Modern music, and particularly the popular American 'ragtime', she believed, had the opposite effect, making the personality 'go to smithereens'.

Mary's belief that folk dance should be neither academic nor pedantic remained unchanged, as did her political allegiances. She was once again looking to promote the healing properties of dance, this time to communities ground down by the experience of war. But the Esperance Club and the Esperance Guild were gone. It would have required enormous resources of time and resolve for her to have single-handedly replicated what had been lost to the war. She now had no professional organisation and no club girls to carry her vision into the world, only her own enthusiasm. Cecil Sharp, on the other hand, had been building his status, travelling in the United States to collect English dances that had taken root there, increasing his resources and repertoire. And he had the backing of the English Folk Dance Society. Unlike Mary's club for working-class youngsters, it had weathered the war. He had a demonstration team, a headquarters and a following of educated and influential men. He was able to classify and codify, to set moves and steps 'in stone', and to establish rules, accreditation processes and a badge system for learners and teachers that could be nationally recognised.

In 1921, Mary found herself with another responsibility. On his death in 1916 she had promised Herbert McIlwaine to take care of his wife, Ethel, and 3-year-old son, Anthony. Five years later Ethel died. Mary adopted Anthony. At 60, she now had responsibility for a young child in a less than comfortable environment; the cottage had a primitive kitchen, no bathroom and no mains water. But despite the hardship, the household in Amberley seems to have been a busy, liberated place shared with cats, a dog, a goat, a rabbit and even a parrot. On one occasion, Emmeline turned up to tea to find Anthony and another young boy that Mary had fostered delivering coal in their best clothes. The following year, Mary moved to the coastal town of Littlehampton so that Anthony could attend school. The town held happy memories for Mary; it was where the Esperance dancers had mixed with newly released and newly recruited suffragettes at the Green Lady hostel. She named their new home in St Flora's Road 'Green Bushes' after a popular folk song.

Mary withdrew from further attempts to rival Sharp. She attended occasional branch meetings of the English Folk Dance Society, where Evelyn Sharp was now playing a more active role, dancing at its summer vacation schools, but she was never involved in its leadership. There was occasional correspondence between the two; in 1921, Sharp attempted a rapprochement, recalling their early collaboration and inviting her to attend an event at which Clive Carey would be singing. He had won the battle for control of the movement and could afford to be conciliatory. Seeking to share responsibility for the 'difference of opinion' between them, he conceded that it was very likely as sincere on her part as on his. Mary was not mollified. She responded but picked him up on discrepancies in his published work, particularly the assertion that it was 'unsafe' to take notation from 'revival' dance sides, when many of the contents of his own first two Morris books had been taken from the Headington side which he had not acknowledged as being a 'revival'. But Sharp was the recognised expert now; within the English Folk Dance Society, Mary was sidelined, her ideas dismissed as aberrations. Her reputation was undermined, quite deliberately, recalled Margaret Dean Smith, who edited the Society's journal in the 1940s. Dean Smith knew the Esperance story well; her father, Arnold Dunbar Smith, was firmly in Mary's activist circle, having designed the cottage in Surrey that the Pethick-Lawrences built for the Esperance girls and she had attended the girls' very first performance at Christmas 1905.

Cecil Sharp did not live to see Mary's 'devastating moment' of revelation about the supposed cause of the rift. He died in 1924. Evelyn wrote in her autobiography:

> I like to remember him moving among the students who loved him and inspiring them with his passion for the dances and songs he had saved, deeply serious about this work of his, yet always ready, with his love of fun, to appreciate a joke. It is a lasting comfort to me to feel that I became a folk dancer before his presence, though never his spirit, was removed from us.

Her comments are a reminder of the generous, inspirational side to Cecil Sharp, that is sometimes forgotten when considering his dealings with Mary.

Evelyn had had little time to involve herself in the dance revival during the pre-war years. But in the 1920s, despite extended fact-finding trips to Germany and stints working with the Friends' famine relief efforts in post-revolutionary Russia, she became very involved in promoting and consolidating her brother's work. In 1925, she and Henry Nevinson attended the vacation dance school in Exeter. The following year, she took on some of the organisation and press work. The couple were regulars at the annual Christmas school in London, which combined classes, lectures and events that she often reviewed. When she was invited to join the management committee of the English Folk Dance Society, she brought an international approach to the revival. In 1927, she danced at the Basque festival in Bayonne with an English team and wrote about it for the *Manchester Guardian*. Her history of dance, *Here We Go Round*, published in 1927, wove her knowledge of English dance with observations on the German dance revival and on the dances of starving peasants in Russia. (Interestingly she glosses over Nellie Chaplin's discovery of Playford's volume which is credited to her brother and gives him a huge amount of credit for discovering lost dances, but her interest is more in the wider history of dance than in the politics of the revival.) She was instrumental in the establishment of Cecil Sharp House and in the 1930s she ran her own dance classes and broadcast on folk dancing for the BBC. The elderly Nevinson toured Canada with the English Folk Dance Society in 1929.

With their radical politics, Evelyn and Nevinson may have seemed unlikely dancers. But they had a pride in English traditions and, as for Mary, dance for Evelyn was political. She was attracted to opportunities for positive cultural exchange and saw hope in the natural exuberance of dance. It would be difficult to go on hating your enemy, she said, if you had to meet him in a dance. Dance suggested to her an international language and understanding – one that she felt politicians might usefully observe. In 1923, she spoke about folk dances as a bond of peace at an event at Westminster Cathedral Hall. Like Mary, and unlike her brother, Evelyn Sharp saw dance as having a radical potential.

The social and cultural development of children and young people had been the focus of Mary's life and she was now drawn into a new youth movement that fellow progressive activists hoped might rival the Scout movement. The Girl Guides had been established at the height of the militant suffragette campaign and had been considered radical by some for offering girls varied life opportunities and promoting outdoor pursuits that were generally thought more suitable for their brothers. But unlike the leaders of the Esperance, early Guide leaders had generally not associated themselves with the campaign for the vote. In the face of socially conservative criticism, they had been careful not to arouse fears that promoting such unladylike activities as hiking might lead young women on to window-breaking and chaining themselves to railings. The newly formed Kindred of the Kibbo Kift, of which Mary became a founder member, was unashamedly progressive and had more in common with the Esperance Club than the Girl Guides.

The First World War had prompted many to question the political classes and international systems of government that had brought Europe to the horrors of the Somme. The Quaker illustrator and novelist John Hargrave was one of them. Hargrave had been a leading Boy Scout leader before the war, touted as a successor to Scouting's founder, Lord Baden-Powell. But his experiences in the war, where he drove ambulances, led to disillusionment with Scouting's officer-class leadership. He came to believe that Scouting's outdoor pursuits were no more than a veneer to militarism. In 1920, he founded a youth movement with a mission to lead the nation to physical and spiritual regeneration. His vision was international and egalitarian; the Kindred of the Kibbo Kift would break down national, gender and class barriers to create a nation and a world free of war, poverty and wasted lives. It is obvious how this would have appealed to Mary and Emmeline, who had struggled all their lives for social equality, women's emancipation, and, more recently, against war. The Kindred was open to both sexes, with women amongst its leadership. Evelyn Sharp, Henry Nevinson and Emmeline were founder members.

The Kindred differentiated themselves from the Scout movement, with whom they shared similar physical and outdoor pursuits such as camping and hiking, with their home-made 'Saxon-inspired' hooded tunics and reverence for the ceremonies of non-European cultures. The leadership looked to primitive societies for spiritual inspiration in a way not dissimilar to Mary's attempts to reconnect with a lost national spirit through the Morris. The Kindred's emphasis on peace and brotherhood attracted pacifists and more socially radical ex-suffragettes. Nor was there any religious bar on membership. Mary and Henry Nevinson sat with Emmeline on the organisation's council and attended its annual 'Althing' or grand council, where Nevinson told tales of his travels in Africa around the campfire. Emmeline hosted Kinsmen at her homes in London and Surrey and Mary offered her cottage for their recuperation and introduced Hargrave to her contacts in the Labour youth movement. The Woodcraft Folk was formed as a breakaway from the Kibbo Kift when Ramsay MacDonald attempted to bring the Kindred into the Labour fold; the Kindred leadership rejected such narrow political and class groupings.

Mary also introduced Hargrave to Rolf Gardiner. A youth member of the Kindred at Cambridge, Gardiner had been a folk dancer whilst a student. Like Mary, he saw dance as a life-giving force with the potential to be harnessed for the public good. Under Gardiner and Mary's influence, the Kindred took up the dance with enthusiasm. For Mary, to see young people dancing must have taken her back to her pre-war days with the Esperance Club. She became close to the charismatic Gardiner, who also found himself at odds with Sharp's control of the movement. In 1922, Gardiner took a party of dancers to Germany to perform. Sharp's sides were now dancing in concert halls, at garden parties and at demonstration venues; Gardiner wanted to see them dancing on village greens. Encouraged by Mary, he went out into the villages of the Cotswolds to learn dances, not from books or classes, but from traditional practitioners. He went into the countryside armed not with a notepad and pencil, but with his whole 'Travelling Morrice' side of dancers who bypassed the observations or contrivances of the academic collector in much the way that Mary's original girls had done. It is not surprising that Mary found his approach appealing.

It was not just Gardiner's practical approach that chimed with Mary. His mystical ideas also coincided with her own belief that the Morris had its roots in religious rituals of pagan times. As she wrote to Clive Carey after Gardiner had stayed with her in Sussex:

He had the real sprit of the Morris as a priest's dance of ritual and discipline. He propounded ideas to me

of what a man's life should be under the influence of
such a ritual which is what I have always held as a wild
dream and idea, but which, had I propounded it to the
average man or woman, would have been voted a silly
old maiden's nonsense! It was rather exciting to have
it all pointed out by a very virile and beautiful youth.

Impressed as she was by Gardiner, she was not unaware of the
irony of her ideas once again being accepted when espoused
by a man.

After Sharp's death, Mary saw her rival lionised as the great
folk revivalist. He had wanted to be recognised as the 'expert'
and in that he had succeeded. Mary's contribution and that
of the Esperance girls slipped out of the English Folk Dance
Society's history. 'The whole story was so garbled that I wonder
the earth did not swallow him up,' she wrote of a lecture on the
history of the dance revival by Douglas Kennedy at a meeting
of the Sussex branch in 1928. That Kennedy saw the revival
from Sharp's perspective was not surprising; he was married
to Helen Karpeles and had been a member of Sharp's pre-war
demonstration side. But he managed to engineer something of
a rapprochement when, as the Society's director, he persuaded
Mary to contribute to the fund to establish a home for the
Society's operations. 'I can't tell you how deeply we appreciate
the gesture you have made and your readiness to let bygones
be bygones,' he wrote. The English Folk Dance Society's new
home was opened in 1930. It was named Cecil Sharp House.

In 1925, Mary suffered something of a breakdown. She was
65 years old and in failing health. She had recently become

the first female magistrate to sit in Sussex, put forward by her local branch of the Labour Party. On being sworn in, she told her audience that she had been instructed not to be influenced by ill will or affection but feared that where young people were concerned she would have to do her best to overcome her affection. She performed the role for twelve years. Her approach was typically practical. She made efforts to reform the juvenile courts, visited offenders in prison and promoted preventative action with local police and families to prevent children getting into trouble with the law in the first place. It was a token of how much she was admired that, when she was ill, a wide-ranging group of supporters, friends and collaborators raised 100 guineas to enable her to rest and recuperate, or, as they put it: to give her 'the gifts of happiness and pleasure to which you have yourself so generously dispensed to many'. Emmeline's family and many of those who had been involved in the mission, suffrage and dance movements contributed, amongst them Katherine Price Hughes and other sisters of the Mission, Esther Knowles, Lady Betty Balfour and her brother Neville Lytton, Nellie Chaplin, Lucy Broadwood, Florrie Warren, Clive Carey, Kenneth Curwen, Frank Kidson, Philip Macer Wright, Nellie and Vic Ghirardi, Max Plowman, A.G. Sayers, Francis Toye, Arnold Dunbar Smith and Edward Carpenter. She had, they told her at a presentation ceremony at Claridge's, 'woven your ideals and your creative work into the fabric of the national community'. Rolf Gardiner spoke of her qualities and achievements alongside Emmeline, Laurence Housman, Neville Lytton and Clive Carey.

By the 1930s, Mary's involvement with the Kibbo Kift, which had offered such hope as an international movement promoting peace and equality, was over. In response to the economic problems of the late 1920s, in the wake of the General Strike and the Wall Street Crash, John Hargrave had transformed the organisation into a more politico-economic movement. The singing and hiking, flowing cloaks and mystical ceremonies by firelight gave way to marching and military style uniforms. Something of an acolyte of the novelist D.H. Lawrence, Rolf Gardiner had turned his back on notions of inclusivity and now espoused some of Lawrence's mystical beliefs in the bonds of masculine brotherhood which he applied to the folk dance movement. He is believed to have encouraged Mary to accept Sharp's conclusion that the Morris was a fundamentally male dance. For despite having worked with Mary and built his career on the work of Esperance Guild, Sharp had eventually come to believe that tradition dictated that Morris sides should be male. At some point during her discussions with Gardiner, Mary suffered a devastating moment of insight into the real reason for the rift between herself and Sharp. It was not as simple as Sharp's contempt for her methods, nor his aversion to the militant suffrage campaign. She had had her suspicions before the war, she recalled in her memoir, but her thoughts had crystalised in her talks with Gardiner:

> Then I realised, in a devastating moment, that these dances were the remains of a purely masculine

ceremonial, and that they represented a ritual of discipline for war and sex expression. I realised that gesture and ritual can be creative and can bring about mental and spiritual experience, and I knew then, for the first time, that by putting women on to this masculine rhythm I had quite innocently and ignorantly broken a law of cosmic ritual and stirred up disharmony which became active as time went on ... I believe now that this ... was the reason for the bitter estrangement between my colleagues and myself, the cause of which was as unknownst to them as it was to me.

There does not seem to be a lot of evidence in Mary's writing before the First World War of any belief that she had upset some natural order and that women should not be dancing. Indeed, though she had acknowledged in print that Morris dances were traditionally performed by men, she had declared her conscience clear at having allowed 'lasses' in her troupe. Old folk, she told the *Somerset Gazette* in 1913, had told her that women had often been allowed to take part. Like Cecil Sharp, she had been influenced by Sir James Frazer and his anthropological study of pagan European cultures. They had both enthusiastically accepted the idea that the dance had its roots in pagan fertility rituals which celebrated the death and renewal of the land. She had suggested that folk songs such as 'John Barleycorn' were about ritual death and rebirth. But in her pieces for *Votes for Women* she had given such songs a particularly female interpretation to support the sacrificial activities of women offering themselves up to prison. Now she apparently believed that she had upset some male 'cosmic' order.

Roy Judge, in his groundbreaking study of the relationship between Sharp and Neal, suggests that the qualms Mary later expressed had never overly bothered her before. But in later life, with Cecil Sharp's followers in control at the English Folk Dance Society, she had to accept that his vision and not that of the Esperance Guild, would be future of the Morris. Judge suggests that Mary could accept Sharp's victory if his way could be seen as representing the natural order of things. Perhaps Gardiner's words enabled her to believe that she had been defeated not by her own failures, or by her dancers' association with radical politics, but by something bigger than herself, a universal (male) spiritual order that she could not contest.

In 1932, the English Folk Dance Society merged with the English Folk Song Society to create the umbrella English Folk Dance and Song Society (EFDSS). The following year, a biography of Cecil Sharp was published by A.H. Fox-Strangeways and Maud Karpeles. The book was critical of some of Sharp's behaviour towards Mary and other collaborators, but in the main it concentrated on Sharp's positive qualities and achievements. Mary commented, a tad bitterly, that she wished she had never seen the other side of him but told Fox-Strangeways that, given his collaborator, she did not think he could have treated her more fairly.

Unsurprisingly, it was Sharp's views on the teaching and history of the Morris that prevailed in the new national society. And in the years that followed, Sharp's belief that the Morris was (and must remain) a purely male, rural tradition was accepted as the orthodoxy. Folk dance societies promulgated this view and less attention was paid to surviving dances that might have undermined confidence in this belief; dances in parts of industrialised north could not be fitted into rural traditions and were often danced by women. In the 1930s, mystical ideas of male brotherhood were espoused across Europe. When the Morris Ring was founded in 1934 to bring together Morris clubs nationwide, its membership was all male. At its inaugural meeting a toast was proposed 'to the memory of the one man above all other to whom we owe our knowledge of the English Morris'. That toast to the 'one man' is still repeated at Ring gatherings. The Morris Ring peddled an attractive national myth of rural pre-Christian societies ritually dancing something that might be recognised as the Morris. The folklorists and anthropologists of the EFDSS and the dancers of the Morris Ring saw themselves as protectors of a national treasure that had been passed down millennia, largely unchanged, from those who would popularise it and degrade it. Not only could women not play a part in supposed male fertility rituals, they were, it was claimed, neither fit enough nor agile enough to dance it, arguments that a glance at the press coverage afforded the Esperance might easily have refuted. And so a dance form that had all but died out until it was revived by a group of young women, led by a campaigner for women's rights, who took that dance and taught it to the nation, now excluded women from mainstream practice.

Mary Neal and her Esperance dancers faded from memory; female dancers did not fit with the new orthodoxy. And memory of the women's involvement in the campaign for the vote only contributed to the desire of the men controlling the folk establishment to forget that they had ever existed. In the post-war period nobody in the folk world wanted to revisit old arguments between their revered leader and the woman who had kick-started the revival. Nor did they want to be reminded of the unsettling days of militancy, raising, as it did, uncomfortable questions about how far it is justifiable for campaigners to go to counter injustice. Women now had the vote. It had, so the orthodoxy claimed, been granted for good behaviour during the war; it suited most of the population to believe that, rather than to ask to what extent the fear of renewed militancy had contributed to government's decision to grant the vote to women. Mary, with her radical associates and commitment to the use of the dance to promote social change, was a complicated figure. Sharp, with his focus solely on 'tradition', did not just fit comfortably within the 'tradition' of all-male dancers; he was also not tainted with radicalism. It was easier for historians of the revival to ignore the complex social and political context of its beginnings, and to credit one man with 'pure' motives with having saved the Morris. The memory of Mary and the slum girls who had taken the Morris across the country faded, just as the memory of Emmeline Pethick-Lawrence, who had taken the WSPU from small band of hopeful pioneers to national political force faded. Cecil Sharp became the face of the Morris, Emmeline Pankhurst the undisputed face of the suffrage movement.

Mary's part in the Morris revival was recognised in 1937 when she was awarded the CBE for her services to English song and dance. Emmeline and Rolf Gardiner spoke at the celebratory lunch at Claridge's. Florrie Warren arrived back in the United Kingdom for a visit, prompting a grand reunion of Esperance dancers at which Florrie danced with Vic Ghirardi, who had once danced on the Esperance's men's side. Mary continued to correspond with old dance practitioners, amongst whom she was remembered fondly, and the following year she was invited to visit the Abingdon Morris men in Stow-on-the-Wold where she showed them her medal. In 1938, Emmeline published her autobiography, *My Part in a Changing World*, which perhaps prompted Mary to address her legacy in *A Tale that is Told*. In anticipation of publication, Laurence Housman wrote the foreword, recalling that he had told Mary after the first Esperance dance display that she should be buried in Westminster Abbey for her achievement. With characteristic wit, she had replied, 'not yet!' She had, he recalled, always kept her humour at the height of the suffrage campaign, when others had lost it.

In 1940, at 80 years old and thirty-five years after she had first seen the Headington dancers, Mary was still writing about the dance. In January, the peace campaigner Max Plowman, a close friend of many years, published her essay 'The Broken Law' in the literary journal *Adelphi*. In it she made public her belief that she had upset the cosmic order in encouraging women to dance. She had, she said once again, discovered evidence, as she went from village to village collecting dances, that the dances were the remains of ancient religious ceremonials and as such they contained references to human and animal sacrifice. In allowing girls to dance to a masculine rhythm she had stirred up disharmony in the folk revival. But with Britain once more at war with Germany, she now drew wider and more specific political conclusions from her own revelation. She had come to believe that her conclusion applied not just to the dance; women were more generally living on a masculine rhythm. Had they not lost their own rhythm, the First World War might have been prevented. And had the 'finer spirits' – by which she presumably means herself, Emmeline and their followers – not resigned from the WSPU in 1912 it might not have become 'openly part of and ruled by the war machine'. Though couched in mystical terms, her words surely reflect the disappointment she shared with Emmeline that women's participation in political life, nationally and on the international stage, had not fulfilled their hopes of preventing war.

Taken out of context, Mary's words seem to indicate that she is turning her back on attempts to claim equality for women and discouraging them from entering into traditionally male spheres of activity. But the article must be seen in the context of European militarism in the 1930s and the outbreak of the Second World War. She was looking to the political situation beyond the dance and her words can be read as suggesting not that women abandon the traditionally male dance (and by implication refrain from attempting to penetrate other bastions of male power and influence) but that they stop trying to emulate male 'rhythms', whether in the dance or the political sphere, and find their own 'rhythm' – one that is not lesser but equal and which will balance the unfettered male power that has led to international conflict. In the face of another war of masculine aggression, she believed that humanity had 'gone as

far as it can under masculine power alone'. The feminine, she
told her readers, must develop in equality or there would be
nothing but destruction. What she meant by this in practical
terms for women – in terms of dance or life more generally
– is not clear. She was influenced by Theosophical concepts
of male and female rhythms that are alien to us now, but
the question of the extent to which women should emulate
male priorities, characteristics and behaviour in search of
equality and agency and to what extent they should attempt
to counterbalance them to the benefit of both men and women
was ahead of its time.

In 1940, Littlehampton was struck by a stray bomb,
probably jettisoned to lighten the bomber's load on the
return run across the Channel. The event brought back
the trauma of Silvertown. Mary left Littlehampton and
joined the Pethick-Lawrences in the growing ex-suffragette
community of Peaslake in Surrey. Emmeline had maintained
a high profile in the years between the wars as a campaigner
for women's educational, legal and employment rights, and
as chairman of the Women's Freedom League. She was now
living in retirement; her husband Fred, now a Labour MP,
was a member of the wartime coalition government. As Lord
Lawrence of Peaslake he would become Attlee's Secretary of
State for India in the Labour government of 1945. For the
last years of her life, Mary lived next door to Emmeline and
took her meals and spent her days with her old friend. The
two elderly campaigners surrounded themselves with an
eclectic collection of 'staff', from secretaries and gardeners
to housekeepers and cooks, all over military age or aliens not

required to contribute directly to the war effort, including a Czech refugee member of the Women's International League for Peace and Freedom.

Mary Neal died in June 1944, aged 85. Emmeline wrote her obituary and read the eulogy at her cremation. She had been amongst the first to enable working people to take country holidays and founded one of the first seaside hostels, but folk song and dance had been her passion:

> To the last day of her life she lost none of her worship of rhythm and beauty, nor did she lose her ardent desire to make them the common heritage of the people. Sensitive to every injustice and to every tragedy she kept a gay and gallant front to life to the very end.

Maud Karpeles wrote an obituary in the *English Folk Dance Journal*. Though appreciative of Mary's contribution, she said that Mary had been mistaken and missed the real significance of the revival. But the revival's significance for Mary was never what it had been for Sharp.

Emmeline was unable to interest publishers in Mary's memoir. It was eventually passed from Anthony McIlwaine, whom Mary had adopted, to Margaret Dean Smith, who made attempts to establish a narrative outlining Mary's place in the dance revival in the 1950s. Her work was followed up by the historian of the dance Roy Dommett in the 1960s. From Margaret Dean Smith the manuscript was returned to Emmeline. On her death it passed to Esther Knowles, the small Esperance dancer who had become Fred Pethick-Lawrence's lifelong secretary, who passed it her niece, Nita Needham, the daughter of Esperance dancers Nellie and Vic Ghirardi. In the 1990s, Needham handed two bags of papers that had belonged to Mary and Emmeline, to Mary's great-great-niece, Lucy Neal.

In the 1970s, second wave feminism – often disparagingly called 'Wimmin's Lib' – coincided with a revived interest in folk music and dance. Thanks to the investigations of Margaret Dean Smith and Roy Dommett, the place of Mary and the Esperance in the dance revival began to be recognised, though it was not until Roy Judge's work in the 1990s that Mary's contribution was fully appreciated. Not only had women been responsible for saving dances from oblivion by collecting them, those same women now provided an argument against those who said that women had never danced and therefore should not dance. Shutting out women, who had done so much to popularise it, men had seized control of the Morris. The women of the 1970s did as the Esperance had done and claimed their right to dance. The Women's Morris Federation was formed in 1975 and Open Morris provided a platform for clubs that wanted to enable men and women to dance together. It was only after a legal challenge under the Equality Act 2010 that the Morris Ring agreed to accept women members. In 2019, when male-only clubs found themselves struggling to recruit, the Ring finally agreed to allow female members to dance.

Ironically, modern Morris sides tend to have more in common with Mary Neal's ethos than Cecil Sharp's. Not only are they inclusive of men and women, they also tend to favour innovation and evolution. Modern dance historians have accepted that the dances were always evolving. Sharp may have won the battle for control of the Morris, but today it is Mary's spirit that is more likely to be referenced by dance sides. The ethos of Islington's New Esperance side (formed in 1973), for example, with its aim of social inclusivity, echoes the spirit of the Esperance. Some modern dancers argue in favour of incorporating modern music trends from popular culture into their repertoires to keep them relevant to modern audiences. Dancers today tend to embrace the long and obscure history of the dance, rather than trying to classify it and pin it down, and to appreciate its links to similar dances in France, Italy and the Basque country. The New Esperance declares a belief in the 'living tradition' of the Morris, accepting change as part of the tradition. Modern dancers embrace input from both men and women in a manner of which surely Mary Neal would have approved. Ultimately, Mary's 'enthusiasm' has trumped Sharp's 'authenticity'.

Mary Neal began the Morris dance revival. For nearly a decade she drove it forward. She strove not for personal gain or achievement but to right the many injustices suffered by women in the years before the First World War, as much through dance as through her militant activism. The early years of the revival coincided with political turmoil. That the Morris revival took off at all was due to her radicalism and involvement in the Labour movement. It was not a coincidence that the Esperance danced at WSPU events or that high-profile suffragettes led the dancers; Mary's commitment to equality and social justice was why she had formed the Esperance and the Esperance Guild. And it was her radicalism that kick-started the Morris revival.

The falling out between Cecil Sharp and Mary Neal has been characterised as one about the practicalities of the dance – accuracy and authenticity versus enthusiasm. But modern folklorists have suggested that despite all the heated words, there was not a huge difference in the styles of dance as taught by Sharp or the Esperance Guild. Mary was always at pains to stress the authenticity and accuracy of her dancers, and Sharp, for all his supposedly scientific approach, was wedded to unproven romantic notions of the origins of the dance, and apt to reject anything that did not fit into his theories of rites and rituals. What really divided Mary Neal and Cecil Sharp was not whether feet should be pointed or legs raised, but their differing convictions about the purpose of the dance and its place in society. Was the Morris a historically accurate performance of an ancient male ritual or a means for women and the dispossessed to lay claim to their own heritage and with it to a place in a society that had marginalised them? The arc of their dispute neatly parallels that of the militant suffrage campaign. Evelyn Sharp thought that but for that, all their exaggerated differences could have been resolved. But Mary's involvement in the militant suffrage campaign that had divided the country sprang from her impulse to change society, to make a place in it for working people and for women, and that impetus was reflected in her approach to the dance. Sharp was scholarly. He wished to record, categorise and to set standards for the performance and teaching of the dances of the past. Mary's interest was not simply in the revival in itself; she saw a radical potential in the dance to transform the lives of the young urban poor. Where he wished to control the dance, and those who danced it, she promoted inclusivity. Folklore was Sharp's career; for Mary it was a means to an end, a way of promoting her socialist, feminist vision.

It is only in recent years that Neal's contribution to the survival of English folk dance, and her attempts to combat the de-humanising effects of urban poverty, have been recognised. Both she and Emmeline have been, to an extent, written out of the popular histories of the movements which would never have got off the ground without their talents and commitment. Mrs Pankhurst dominates the history of the militant suffrage movement as Cecil Sharp does the world of folk dance. And in both cases the reasons for the rifts have been misrepresented; Emmeline's withdrawal from the WSPU was deliberately misrepresented for decades as being rooted in policy differences about the wisdom of increasingly militant tactics; really it was rooted in personality issues and the practicalities of Fred and Emmeline's wealth potentially being used as a weapon against the militant movement. The rift between Neal and Sharp was as much about personal ambition and his loathing of militancy as it was about authenticity and accuracy. The rift in the WSPU and the rift in the dance movement were parallel and linked.

Gradually, the contributions of both women are being recognised. Streets have been named after both Mary and Emmeline in Littlehampton to mark the place where folk dancers brought the suffragettes one of their most influential recruits. Mary's home in Littlehampton and Emmeline's in Holmwood, Surrey, are both now marked with blue plaques. And in Islington, the New Esperance women's Morris side recognises the contribution of the dancers after whom they are named, branding themselves in the purple, white, green and gold of the WSPU and the United Suffragists.

It was militant suffragettes who returned the forgotten dances to the people of England. Mary Neal, Emmeline Pethick-Lawrence, Lady Constance Lytton, Evelyn Sharp, Laurence Housman, Mabel Tuke, May Start, Lady Isabel Margesson, Blanche Payling, Florrie Warren, Esther Knowles and the girls of the Esperance all played a key role in re-establishing the Morris as a living dance form that is practised all over England to this day, rather than one encountered only in academic journals and history books. And the impetus to do so came from their commitment to change society for the better, the same impetus that drove them to militant action and to prison.

Bibliography

Published material

Atherton, Kathryn, *Suffragette Planners and Plotters: the Pankhurst, Pethick-Lawrence Story*, 2019

Atherton, Kathy, *Suffragettes, Suffragists and Antis: the fight for the vote in the Surrey Hills*, 2017

Balfour, Lady Betty, ed., *Letters of Constance Lytton*, 1925

Boyes, Georgina, *The Imagined Village: Culture, Ideology and the English Folk Revival*, 1993

Buckley, R.R. and Neal, Mary, *The Shakespeare Revival and the Stratford-upon-Avon Movement*, 1911

Camden History Society, *The Streets of St Pancras: Somers Town and the Railway Lands*, 2020

Chandler, Keith, *Ribbons, Bells and Squeaking Fiddles*, 1993

Cowman, Krista, *Women of the Right Spirit: Paid Organisers of the WSPU*, 2007

Crawford, Elizabeth, *The Women's Suffrage Movement: A Reference Guide 1866–1928*, 1999

Crawford, Elizabeth, *The Women's Suffrage Movement in Britain and Ireland*, 2006

Cutting, John, *History and the Morris Dance: A Look at Morris Dancing from its Earliest Days until 1850*, 2005

Drakeford, Mark, *Social Movements and their Supporters: The Green Shirts in England*, 1997

Forrest, John, *Morris and Matachin: A Study in Comparative Choreography*, 1984

Fox-Strangeways, A.H., *Cecil Sharp*, 1935

Garland, M.A., '*It's Street theatre really!*': *A History of Cotswold Morris Dancing in the Twentieth Century*, 2018

Hobsbawn, Eric and Ranger, Terence (ed.), *The Invention of Tradition*, 2009

Howkins, Alun, 'The Discovery of Rural England', *Englishness: Politics and Culture 1880–1920* ed. Colls, R. and Dodd, P., 1986

John, Angela V., *Evelyn Sharp Rebel Woman, 1869–1955*, 2009

Judge, Roy, 'Mary Neal and the Esperance Morris', *Folk Music Journal* 5 (5), 1989

Karpeles, Maud, *Cecil Sharp: His Life and Work*, 1967

Knevett, Arthur, 'The Folk Dance Movement: Mary Neal, Cecil Sharp and the Struggle for Supremacy', *Musical Traditions*, 2019

Liddington, Jill, *The Militant Suffrage Movement: Citizenship and Resistance in Britain*, 2003

Liddington, Jill and Norris, Jill, *One Hand Tied Behind Us: The Women's Suffrage Movement*, 2000

Lowe, Barbara, 'Early Records of the Morris in England', *Journal of the EFDSS* 8 (2),1957

Lytton, Lady Constance, *Prisons and Prisoners*, 1914

Kenney, Annie, *Memories of a Militant*, 1924

Kidson, Frank and Neal, Mary, *English Folk-Song and Dance*, 1915

Mackenzie, Midge, *Shoulder to Shoulder*, London, 1975

Mangan, J.A. (ed.), *Making Imperial Mentalities: Socialisation and British Imperialism*, 2014

Martz, Linda, 'Mary Neal and Emmeline Pethick: from mission to activism', *Women's History Review* 23 (4), 2014

Montagu, Lily, *My Club and I*, 1941

Neal, Mary, *Dear Mother Earth*, 1900

Neal, Mary, *The Esperance Morris Book part 1: A Manual of Morris Dances, Folk-Songs and Singing Games*, 1910

Neal, Mary, *The Esperance Morris Book part 2: Morris Dances, Country Dances, Sword Dances and Sea Shanties*, 1911

Pankhurst, Christabel, *Unshackled*, 1959

Pankhurst, Emmeline, *My Own Story*, 1914

Pankhurst, E. Sylvia, *The Suffragette Movement*, 1931

Pethick-Lawrence, Emmeline, *My Part in a Changing World*, 1938

Pethick-Lawrence, Emmeline, 'Working Girls Clubs', *University Social Settlements*, ed. Reason, Will, 1898

Pethick-Lawrence, Frederick, *Fate has been Kind*, 1942

Pugh, Martin, *The Pankhursts*, 2001

Pugh, Martin, *Votes for Women in Britain 1867–1928*, 1994

Purvis, June, *Emmeline Pankhurst*, 2002

Purvis, June, *Christabel Pankhurst: A Biography*, 2018

Ross, Ellen, 'St Francis in Soho: Emmeline Pethick, Mary Neal, the West London Methodist Mission, and the Allure of "Simple Living" in the 1890s', *Church History* 83 (4), 2014

Salter, Mike, *All About the Morris*, 2014

Sharp, Evelyn, *Here We Go Round*, 1927

Sharp, Evelyn, *Unfinished Adventure*, 1936

Sherwell, Arthur, *Life in West London: A Study and a Contrast*, 1897

Tickner, Lisa, *The Spectacle of Women: Imagery of the Suffrage Campaign 1907–14*, 1987

Walkowitz, Daniel J., *City Folk: English Country Dance and the Politics of the Folk in Modern America*, 2010

Wickstead, Helen, 'Wild Worship of a Lost and Buried Past: Enchanted Archaeologies and the Cult of Kata, 1908–1924', *Bulletin of the History of Archaeology*, 27(1), 2017

Wortley, Russell, 'An Esperance Club meeting at the Red House, Ascot c1910', *The Cotswold Morris: Hey Dey, Decline and Revival*, 1980

Archive material

Advance – the journal of the West London Mission

Booth, Charles, 'Poverty Maps and Notebooks', London School of Economics

Dommett, Roy, *How did you think it was?* 1980

Dove, Iris, 'Sisterhood or Surveillance? The Development of Working Girls' Clubs in London 1880–1939', thesis 1996

Harrison, Brian, 'Suffragette interview collection, the Women's Library', London School of Economics

Holmwood Parish Magazine 1891–1914

Kibbo Kift archive, London School of Economics Library

Neal, Mary, Papers, including 'A Tale that is Told – the autobiography of a Victorian Woman', 1937–9, Vaughan Williams Memorial Library, Cecil Sharp House

Pethick-Lawrence, Emmeline, Letter Collection, the Women's Library, London School of Economics

Pethick-Lawrence, Frederick and Emmeline, Papers, Trinity College, Cambridge

Ross, Ellen, 'Disgruntled Missionaries: The Friendship of Mary Neal and Emmeline Pethick-Lawrence at the West London Mission', Ramapo College of New Jersey, 2009

Sharp, Evelyn and Nevinson, Henry, Letter collection, Bodleian Library, Oxford

Votes for Women magazine, Royal Holloway archive

Various local and national newspapers

Index